Theological Questions

Analysis and Argument

Theological Questions

Analysis and Argument

by

Owen C. Thomas

Morehouse-Barlow Co., Inc.
Wilton, Connecticut 06897

Morehouse-Barlow Co., Inc.
78 Danbury Road
Wilton, Connecticut 06897

ISBN 0-8192-1328-4

Library of Congress Catalog Card Number 83-60658

Printed in the United States of America

To the Faculty, Students and Staff
of the
Episcopal Theological School
1952–1974
and of the
Episcopal Divinity School
1974–1982

Contents

Preface

This volume is a sequel to my book *Introduction to Theology.* * In that book I presented the traditional topics of Christian theology, and I suggested that students focus on the analysis and resolution of specific theological questions associated with these topics. At the end of each chapter I listed a number of questions which had occurred to me in working on the topic of the chapter. I suggested, however, that students should work on questions which had actually arisen in their own lives and work. In the course in which I used that volume a large part of the class time was devoted to the presentation and discussion of student papers on such questions. My objective was to give students some guided practice in the analysis, clarification, and resolution of theological questions which were of real interest to them. In many of my lectures I attempted to exemplify a method for carrying this out. The present volume consists of some of these lectures.

Since I have found no discussion of theological method aimed specifically at the analysis, clarification, and resolution of specific theological questions, I have presented the outline and rationale of such a method in chapter 1 and the appendix. In the intervening chapters I have attempted to exemplify this method in the treatment of questions related to each of the topics addressed in the first volume. Most of the questions are in fact taken from those listed in that volume.

I believe, and my experience over the past ten years has confirmed, that this is a method which can be taught, learned and used. I have found that when students gain some practice in such a method, it can be a very liberating experience. They suddenly realize to their amazement that they can do theology themselves. They had been overawed by reading the great theological systems and treatises. Doing theology meant the writing of such systems and treatises. This they believed was clearly beyond them.

However, through learning and using some such method as the one I have tried to exemplify here, students can gain a real sense of accomplishment. Since they can use this method on the questions about which they are really curious or troubled, they can gain a new understanding of the

*Wilton, Ct: Morehouse-Barlow Co., Inc., 1983. This volume will be referred to as *Introduction* or "the text".

relevance of theology to their lives and their work. For here is a method which they can use and perfect for the rest of their lives without direct dependence upon their teachers. This, I believe, is one of the main purposes of the study of theology.

I have received many helpful comments on parts of this book from the faculty and students of the Episcopal Divinity School, the North American College in Rome, and the members of the Boston Theological Society, but of course the responsibility for the views presented is entirely my own. In particular my colleague Professor Daniel B. Stevick offered a number of valuable suggestions on chapters 18 and 19. Also I want to express my gratitude to my wife, Professor Margaret R. Miles of the Harvard Divinity School, for many delightful and illuminating conversations on topics historical, theological and existential.

Owen C. Thomas
Rome
December, 1982

1

The Locus and Method of Theology[1]

As I have read theological books and journals over the past few decades I have often had the impression that Christian theology was simply an intellectual or academic game without serious purpose or serious effect on the thinking or action of anyone, in particular Christians and the church. To be sure it is often a fascinating game and supplies many of us with a living, but it claims to be more than that. Can it maintain this claim? Is there any real point or necessity to theology? More specifically what is the true locus of theology? Where does it need to be done, not as a game but of necessity?

I want to suggest that the primary locus of theology is the life and work of Christians, both their private and their public lives, in the church and in the world. I would argue that the fundamental beginning point of theology is simply the questions, the issues, and the problems which arise in the life and work of Christians and in their communal life in the church. This is where theology becomes a necessity and not merely a hobby or a game. Has it not always been so? Was this not the case with the biblical and the early Christian authors?

One of the major issues in the lives of the earliest Christians was the crucifixion of the Messiah. This was not supposed to happen. The Messiah of Israel was supposed to lead Israel to victory against its enemies and usher in a new era of peace, justice and prosperity. So what in God's name is going on? The first Christians resolved this issue in various ways. They interpreted Jesus' death as a sacrifice for sins on the analogy of Old Testament sacrifice, or as a victorious struggle with the powers of evil, or as an example of humble obedience to the divine will. This was some of the first theology that the Christian community was called upon to do.

Other issues with which the early Christians had to deal concerned food offered to idols, ecstatic phenomena, the relation to governing authorities, and marriage and divorce. A classic paradigm of the emergence of theology was the issue of what to do with gentile converts. Should they be subjected to circumcision and the food laws or not? This was a forced decision; the church had to go one way or the other; it could not ignore the issue. There was a debate and arguments on both sides. Paul takes up the issue in the letter to the Galatians and makes an extended argument against subjection to the law and in favor of justification by grace through faith. This was a critical turning point in the history of the church, in its self-understanding and in its relation to Judaism. And the road it took was the result of argument and decision on a theological issue.

Later the task of instruction, the explication of the developing rule of faith, and the treatment of more speculative issues raised by contemporary Middle Platonism led naturally to the writing of more extended and systematic treatments of the topics of Christian faith. This issued in works such as Irenaeus' *The Demonstration of the Apostolic Preaching* and Origen's *On First Principles,* later in the medieval summae, and ultimately in the massive theological systems of the seventeenth to the twentieth centuries. This type of theological writing, which has been in such vogue until recently, had two results. The first was to obscure the fact that theology arose as the attempt to clarify and resolve the issues arising in the life and work of Christians. The second was to turn the study of theology into the study of these great systems, that is, into the study of the results of theological reflection rather than the actual carrying out of theological reflection itself. To be sure the study of the great systems provided a framework within which the specific issues could be approached, but it did not offer a method for dealing with these issues.

My purpose in the course referred to in the preface and in this volume is to turn this development around. I want to turn the study of theology away from the systems and back to the issues which have always been the starting point of theology. Then the systems may often serve as reference works in the analysis and resolution of the issues.

This purpose has raised for me in a new way the question of theological method. Most of the writing about theological method in this century has dealt with the method of interpreting historical texts (Bultmann, et al.), or with the method of developing a theological system (Tillich), or with theological method in only the most general sense (Lonergan, Tracy). As we shall see, aspects of this writing on method will be useful at various points in treating specific theological issues, but very little of it deals with the method of identifying, clarifying, and resolving of such issues. This is one reason why much occasional writing on specific theological issues is marked by a lack of methodological clarity and is based on intuition, an anachronistic mining of scripture and tradition, and the use of various illegitimate rhetorical devices.

Thus I have been searching for and attempting to develop an analytical method which would be appropriate for dealing with specific theological issues. Of course analytical methods are not new in theology. One version was broached in the dialogue method of Justin and Anselm. Another was brought to a fine systematic elegance in the method of Aquinas with its questions, articles, objections, and responses. His method is formally similar to the kind of method I am seeking, and I have borrowed and modernized some of its elements, as will be seen below in the employment of analysis, definition, distinction, proof, and so forth.

Analytical method in theology received a modern impetus in Hume's writings on natural religion, miracles, providence, and immortality. The analytical tradition deriving from Hume was deepened and expanded in this century by the work of Russell, Moore, Wittgenstein, Ayer, and others. A later form of this tradition, which was called linguistic analysis, began to be applied to theological questions about 1950.[2] With a few exceptions these attempts were mostly single essays and were not very reflective on the method of approach to theological issues. However, they exemplified an analytical method in theology and thus offered a model for further work.

Although this literature does not offer a clear-cut method for theological analysis, it does offer a series of important examples, hints, and some rules of thumb. The closest approach to a specific method of analysis can be found in John Wilson's book *Thinking with Concepts*.[3] He offers nine specific techniques for conceptual analysis which can be applied as successive steps in the analysis of questions: model cases, contrary cases, related cases, borderline cases, invented cases, social context, underlying anxiety, practical results, and results in language.

It is perhaps too much to expect a detailed and clear-cut statement of method in this area. In a somewhat different context Karl Popper has stated:

> There is no method peculiar to philosophy. . . . And yet, I am quite ready to admit that there is a method which might be described as "the one method of philosophy." But it is not characteristic of philosophy alone; it is, rather, the one method of all *rational discussion,* and therefore of the natural sciences as well as of philosophy. The method I have in mind is that of stating one's problem clearly and of examining its various proposed solutions critically.[4]

In the appendix I outline a practical method for the clarification, analysis, and resolution of specific theological issues. At this point I shall comment on some aspects of theological method which require some further exploration.

One of the first steps in theological method is to determine whether a particular issues is theological or of some other kind, such as historical, factual, psychological, or strategic. I would suggest that a theological issue is one which inquires about God or about the relation of the creation or some part of it to God. Tillich puts this in a somewhat different way in his first formal criterion of theology. "Only those propositions are theological which deal with their object in so far as it can become a matter of ultimate concern for us."[5] This prevents the interference of theology in other disciplines and vice versa. In particular it prevents the use of theology to answer historical or scientific questions or vice versa. We shall see, for example, that it is not immediately clear whether or not the questions discussed in chapters 3, 8 and 15 are theological issues.

One aspect of theological method which is often ignored in contemporary discussions is that of theological argument. Theology does not consist simply of assertions or propositions. It is not simply confession of faith, although a good deal of contemporary theology seems to be just that. It involves the giving of reasons, evidence, grounds, or proof for its statements. Theology involves argument for its assertions by offering some kind of basis for accepting them over against alternative assertions.

Philosophy from the beginning has been concerned with the nature of valid argument, but through the influence of Aristotle it has focussed on deductive and inductive argument and in modern times especially on the most rigorous forms of these. Deductive argument has played a relatively small part in theology. It has sometimes been used to demonstrate the inconsistency of opposing views, but theology has hardly ever been presented as a system in which the propositions are deduced from axioms or premises. Most theological argument has involved appeal to scripture, tradition or experience. This could be described as inductive in the most general sense. However, the philosophical analysis of induction has been developed primarily in connection with the natural sciences where the focus is on sense experience, and as a result it has little if any application to theology.

Thus Aristotle's original ideal for logic as a formal science has more and more led the study of logic and argument away from its everyday use in law, politics, commerce, morals, and religion. The result has been that theology has had to fend for itself in finding appropriate ways of arguing its points. The most common form of theological argument has been the appeal to scripture and to tradition in the form of the rule of faith, concilear decisions, liturgical forms, and the assertions of theologians. This is an appeal to authority, and modern studies of logic treat this form of argument only rarely. And when they do, it is usually under the heading of "weak" forms of argument along with analogy and abduction.

From the beginning theology had another much more practical resource for guidance in the development of its arguments, and that was rhetoric, the art of persuasive discourse. The apologists and theologians of the early centuries studied the rhetorical tradition, often were rhetors or teachers of rhetoric (for example, Gregory Nazianzen, Cyprian, and Augustine), and often employed rhetorical methods, styles, and devices. The study of rhetoric was always an essential ingredient of classical education. Along with logic and grammar, it formed the trivium of the medieval seven liberal arts, and it was an important element in liberal education down through the nineteenth century.

From the time of the Renaissance, however, there was a steady decline in the intellectual status of rhetoric. It came increasingly to be identified with its stylistic and decorative aspects and with its purposes of entertainment. One of the last great works written by a theologian in a consciously rhetorical style is Schleiermacher's *On Religion: Speeches to the Cultured among its Despisers* (1799). Today our ordinary usage of the term rhetoric is entirely pejorative, and no theologian in this century has evidenced any knowledge of it. (I believe that Walter J. Ong is the only exception to this.) This is a serious loss to contemporary theology, because it lacks clarity and order in regard to its arguments. Theologians today need to become a lot more self-conscious about how they are arguing and about the various modes of argument open to them. Lacking this they tend to fall into forms of argument which are inappropriate in theology.

A major contribution in this area is Stephen E. Toulmin's book *The Uses of Argument*[6] which holds a unique position in the history of logic and rhetoric. Toulmin criticizes the logical tradition for its lack of concern for the forms of arguments in the everyday life of the world. He develops a pattern of informal argument based on a jurisprudential model which he believes is useful for the analysis of actual arguments on concrete matters. It is interesting to note that while Toulmin betrays no knowledge of the rhetorical tradition, contemporary rhetoricians have hailed his work as a major contribution to their discipline, and theologians have seized upon his pattern for the analysis of theological argument.[7]

Toulmin depicts his analysis of the layout of an argument in the following way:[8]

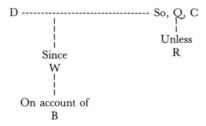

And he gives this example:

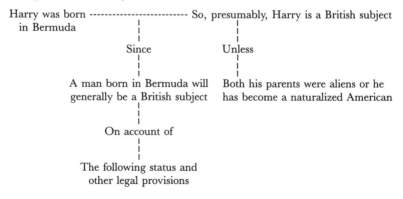

The conclusion (C) of an argument takes the form of a claim or an assertion. About any conclusion it can be asked, What is the basis of your conclusion? On what grounds do you make this claim? The answer to this question is given in the form of data (D). The data can be of a variety of logical types: statements of historical facts, reports of observations, and so forth, depending upon the field of argument.

About this move from data to conclusion it can be asked, Why do these data justify this conclusion? The answer to this question is given in the form of a rule or inference license or warrant (W). Warrants are general hypothetical statements which authorize the move from data to conclusion. They may be left implicit, but they are always at least implicit, because they determine the kind of data which are relevant to the conclusion. About any warrant it can be asked, On what basis can you assert this? What are the grounds for this warrant? The answer to this kind of question is given in the form of backing (B) for the warrant.

About any warrant with its backing it can be asked, What degree of force or probability does it confer on your conclusion? The answer to this question is given in the form of a qualifier (Q) such as "necessarily" or "probably." Finally, about the conclusion and its qualifier the question can be asked, Are there any exceptions to this conclusion or circumstances in which the conclusion does not hold? The answer to this kind of question is given in the form of rebuttals (R).

Toulmin's pattern of informal argument can be used as a guide in analyzing and developing theological arguments. The most common form of theological argument in Christian history has been the appeal to scripture. The New Testament authors appealed to the Old Testament, and the early Christian authors began to appeal to both. Since I argue in the text that the norm of theological assertions is the revelation of God attested in the Bible, I want to focus on this type of argument in particular. A major contribution to the analysis of arguments involving the appeal to scripture has been made by David H. Kelsey in his book *The Uses of Scripture in Recent Theology.* His interpretation can be summarized in the following way.

The way the Bible is used in theology is dependent first of all upon an imaginative characterization of the nature of Christian faith as a whole and how it becomes a reality in people's lives. This characterization, of course, may be derived from or be inspired by the Bible. This is turn determines the variety of ways in which the Bible is used authoritatively in the church's common life to mediate the presence of God for the shaping and transforming of people's lives. The use of the Bible to authorize theological proposals is just one element in this larger whole.

Then Kelsey proceeds to use Toulmin's pattern of informal argument to analyze the ways in which the Bible can be used to authorize theological proposals. It can be used as data, warrant or backing or as the basis of any of these. This means that the Bible can be used in six logically distinct ways to authorize a theological proposal. The Bible is rarely used directly for this purpose, that is, the use of specific biblical texts as data or warrant is rare. Kelsey gives the example of B. B. Warfield's argument from 2 Timothy 3:16 to the plenary inspiration of the Bible.[9]

A further complication noted by Kelsey is that in the more usual case in which the Bible is used as the basis of the data, these data are related to the Bible in a number of quite distinct ways based on different ways of construing what is the authoritative aspect of the Bible. For example, the authoritative aspect of the Bible may be construed to be its doctrinal or conceptual content, its recital or narrative character, or its mythic or symbolic expression of a saving event. Presumably different parts of the Bible should be construed in different ways. The import of Kelsey's analysis is that an appeal to the Bible to authorize a theological proposal is not a simple matter but rather involves a number of complex judgments and decisions.

It is clear that Kelsey has raised a number of fundamental issues which have to be faced and resolved by anyone like myself who appeals to the Bible to authorize theological proposals. It would, however, require a separate volume to carry this out in detail. All that can be done at this point is to outline the way in which these issues might be resolved. Since Kelsey focuses much of his criticism on the general way in which I have presented the appeal to the Bible in chapters 2 and 3 of the text, the simplest way to proceed is to respond to this criticism.

My main thesis in the text is that the fundamental authority for theology is the revelation of God attested in the Bible. The Bible consists largely of narrative, the interpretation of the meaning of this narrative, and commentary on this and on its significance for human life. The authors of the Bible recount events and interpret them as events in which God is acting to reveal the divine nature and will and to accomplish salvation. (Some of these events are mythological, some legendary, and some historical in roughly the modern sense.) Thus the Bible represents the first written deposit of the original testimony to the revelation of God culminating in Christ. The aim of the historical critical theological interpretation of the Bible is to determine what the original authors and their editors intended to say about God and the world in relation to God in their own terms and in their own day and the possible consensus of these meanings. Then the task of theology is to express this consensus in language which is intelligible to and affirmable by modern people.

This view is one version of what Kelsey describes as the "standard picture" of the relation of scripture and theology.[10] In this view the Bible is understood to preserve the content of revelation. Since the task of theology is seen to be the elucidation of revelation, then theological assertions are understood as "translations" of biblical meanings. This assumes that there is a continuity of concept and meaning between the Bible and theology. Kelsey believes that this assumption is false and offers three objections.

First, this metaphorical use of "translation" stretches the concept into unintelligibility and obscures the possibility of conceptual discontinuity. Furthermore, it is logically impossible to translate from one conceptuality to another. This is properly called redescription. I would point out, however, that "translation" is being used as a metaphor, and it is a good and quite intelligible metaphor for redescription.

Secondly, Kelsey states that the metaphorical use of "translate" assumes a continuity of meaning between a scriptural text and a theological proposal. He quotes D. E. Nineham: "Many statements in ancient texts have *no* meaning today in any normal sense of the word 'meaning.' "[11] However, the "standard picture" does not require that all biblical texts have significant meaning but only that some do. Kelsey and Nineham are not denying this.

Thirdly, Kelsey argues that "translation" is not an adequate metaphor for the indirect way in which some theologians actually bring scripture to bear on their theological proposals. The metaphor of "translation" fits only three (I would say four) out of the seven case studies he presents. This, however, is an objection against translation as a formal description of how all theologians actually use scripture, and the validity of the metaphor does not depend upon its fulfilling this function.

So I conclude that Kelsey's objections against the "standard picture" and thus against my view are not persuasive. His alternative to the "standard picture" is that scripture is authority for theology in that it "provides patterns determinate enough to *function* as the basis for the assessment of the Christian aptness" of theological proposals.[12] This certainly includes the "standard picture" and in that sense justifies it.

The nature of the authority of the Bible, however, need not be stated as schematically as it is in the text, and it need not be as sharply focussed on the concept of revelation. The description of the Bible as testimony to revelation may be too narrow and may tend to belie the variety found in the Bible. A better way to put it might be to say that the people of God over a millenium and more came to know and believe in God and live before God in particular ways. They wrote about this in a variety of ways:

> "stories of God's acts in the past, general historical memories, pieces of cosmology and geography, personal reminiscences, speeches of holy men and stories about them, lists and genealogies, hymns and folk-poetry, groups of observations on 'Wisdom,' i.e., general matters of morality and manners."[13]

Furthermore, these traditions were constantly reinterpreted. In and through these writings the authors and editors said and implied certain things about God and about the world and especially humanity in relation to God. These sayings and implications constitute a broad consensus about God and the world in relation to God which culminates in and is focussed on Jesus. The existence, nature, and breadth of this consensus is debatable in the discipline of historical critical theological exegesis. The task of theology is to offer an interpretation of God and the world in relation to God which is coherent with some version of this consensus. This version functions as the basis for the assessment of theological proposals.

I should point out, however, that the following essays will stress analysis rather than argument, and this for two reasons. First, the arguments will depend primarily upon biblical exegesis and historical interpretation, and I am neither an exegete nor an historian. Secondly, a full theological argument on most of the questions addressed would have to be of book length. Therefore, the arguments in the following essays will consist of sketches or outlines of the points which might be made. References to particular biblical passages and historical authors will constitute indications of the places where detailed exegesis and historical interpretation are required for the completion of the argument. For this reason I do not put any great stock in the conclusions I come to in these essays, since I am mainly concerned to exemplify a *method* of analysis and argument rather than to present a particular series of conclusions. The conclusions may be wrong, but my thesis is that the only way to determine this is through a more careful and thorough pursuit of the method I am proposing.

I should also note that the essays vary a good deal in length, and some are more fully documented than others. This derives from the fact that some questions require more analysis than others, and some are addressed more often and more fully than others in the Bible, the Christian tradition, and in contemporary theology.

Finally, I have often noted that theologians, especially those who believe that they have a reputation to defend, avoid issues which they cannot resolve. (I have noticed this much more in this century than in previous ones. Perhaps this is due to the influence of the media.) Have you ever read a theologian stating that he or she is at a loss as to how to resolve some particular theological issue? I never have, nor have I ever written it myself. It takes a measure of greatness and humility to make such a statement. However, it is usually quite obvious to the reader when a theologian is avoiding an issue. I am sure there are examples in my own writing.

My point is that this tendency derives at least in part from lack of clarity in regard to the appropriate method for dealing with specific theological issues. If theologians were clearer about such a method, then at least they could indicate clearly how far they were able to proceed with this method, where they were stuck and why. This would at least open up the possibility for others to build on their work and make further progress. I shall make every effort to practice what I have been teaching.

In this connection it is worth noting that many of the issues addressed in the following essays are ones which other theologians have avoided presumably because of their difficulty. If this is the case, then they should be a good test of the method which is being proposed.

2

Revelation

Which comes first, faith or revelation?

This question arises because we often hear statements about revelation and faith which seem to be contradictory. For example, on the one hand it is often said that it is revelation which makes faith possible, or that apart from revelation we could not know anything about God and thus have faith. On the other hand, it is sometimes said that revelation can only be received by faith, that apart from faith the experience of revelation would be interpreted as something else, such as an eruption from the unconscious, the voice of conscience, or the pressure of society. Do we have faith in God and thus are able to perceive and receive God's revelation when it occurs in our life and experience? Or is it rather the case that we know nothing of God until God is present to us in revelation and then we can respond in faith? Which comes first, faith or revelation?

Let us interpret "faith" to mean the human attitude and relationship to God of trust, love, and obedience. By "revelation" let us understand God's self-disclosure to humanity on the analogy of human self-disclosure. If revelation were understood to include the human perceiving of it by faith, then the question would be answered by definition. Faith and revelation would be correlative and presuppose each other.

Something can "come first" in relation to something else logically, temporally, or in regard to value or importance. It is important to be clear about which meaning we are attributing to this phrase, because the answer might be different for each meaning. Let us interpret it to mean coming first logically in the sense of being the basis or presupposition of something else. Coming first logically may also involve coming first temporally, but not necessarily. Now the question can be rephrased: Which is the basis or presupposition of the other, faith or revelation? The possible answers to this question are as follows:

1. Revelation is the presupposition of faith.
2. Faith is the presupposition of revelation.
3. Faith and revelation are correlative and presuppose each other.
4. Faith is the presupposition of revelation, but revelation transforms and perfects faith.

Our procedure will be to investigate the Bible and the tradition on this question and then to determine which answer best accords with the results of this investigation.

Let us look at some of the classical occasions of revelation in the Bible. Jacob's dream at Bethel (Gen. 28:10-22; see 35:7) presupposes some faith in God, but the revelation of God in the dream strengthens and deepens his faith and leads him to make a specific commitment to God. Similarly before the burning bush episode (Ex. 3:1-14) Moses, although he had been raised in Pharaoh's household, knew that he was a Hebrew and presumably had a rudimentary faith in their God. However, in the revelation of God at the bush he learns God's name, accepts God's call, and his faith is clarified and deepened. In the case of the revelation of God to Samuel (1 Sam. 3:1-15) he is depicted as a boy who had been dedicated to God by his mother as an infant, who had ministered to the Lord in the sanctuary at Shiloh, but who did not yet know the Lord and to whom the word of the Lord had not yet been revealed. Through this revelation, however, Samuel became a prophet who spoke the word of the Lord. "The Lord revealed himself to Samuel at Shiloh by the word of the Lord. And the word of Samuel came to all Israel" (3:21-4:1). So this is a case of rudimentary faith being transformed by revelation into the mature faith of the prophet. Isaiah's vision in the temple (Isa. 6:1-8) again presupposes faith, but in the revelation through this vision Isaiah is moved to repentance, responds to God's call, and thus his faith is deepened.

Peter's confession at Caesarea Philippi (Mk. 8:27-30 par) presupposes Jewish faith and some kind of inchoate faith in Jesus, but in response to Jesus' question Peter confesses his faith in Jesus as Messiah. According to Matthew Jesus responds, "Blessed are you, Simon Bar-Jona! For flesh and blood has not revealed this to you, but my Father who is heaven" (Mt. 16:17). The resurrection appearance on the road to Emmaus (Lk. 24:13-35) is a case of Jewish faith plus disappointed faith in Jesus being transformed by the revelation of the risen Christ into nascent Christian faith. "He was known to them in the breaking of bread" (v. 35).

Paul's conversion involves zealous Jewish faith (Gal. 1:14; Acts 22:3) being transformed into equally zealous Christian faith through what Paul describes as God's being "pleased to reveal his son to me" (Gal. 1:16). The conversion of Cornelius, the God-fearing gentile, represents the transformation of peripheral Jewish faith into Christian Faith through the preaching of Peter and the gift of the Holy Spirit (Acts 10). The preaching of Paul on the Areopagus moves some to turn from faith in pagan gods to Christian faith (Acts 17:22-34; see 1 Thess. 1:9). In summary, the Bible seems to support the fourth answer, that faith is the presupposition of revelation but that revelation transforms and perfects faith. This transformed faith is the response to the revelation, but it is preceded by a different or more rudimentary faith.

In the tradition revelation soon came to be understood as the divine disclosure of true doctrine and faith as belief in or assent to this doctrine. Thus the tradition was operating with different definitions of faith and revelation and was not treating the question as formulated above. Justin Martyr, Clement of Alexandria, and Augustine held that the pagan philosophers believed some true doctrine before hearing the gospel, but that the revelation in the Bible supplemented and completed this when it was assented to by faith. Thomas Aquinas summarized this view by asserting that there was a natural knowledge of God which could be achieved by unaided natural reason and which therefore did not require revelation or faith, and also a revealed knowledge of God which was given in the Bible and which could be assented only by faith. He taught that a person's faith was caused by having revelation proposed to it and by being inwardly moved to assent by divine grace.[1] With these different definitions of faith and revelation this part of the tradition supports the first answer, that revelation is the presupposition of faith.

At the Reformation there was a partial recovery of the biblical understanding of the relation of revelation and faith. By the seventeenth century, however, this had been lost and the traditional view took over again. In this century there has been a recovery of the views of the Bible and the Reformers. In the extreme form of this recovery (Barth) it is asserted that revelation is the presupposition of faith and creates faith. In the more moderate forms (Brunner, Tillich, Baillie, Temple) it is affirmed that apart from the special revelation attested in the Bible there is a general or universal revelation in the creation and in human reason and conscience the reception of which involves a rudimentary kind of faith. Then this rudimentary faith is the basis for receiving the special revelation. In summary, there is no consensus in the tradition on this issue, but what there is tends to support the first answer.

When the Bible and the tradition are in conflict on an issue, we must side with the Bible, especially in this case in which the tradition is not clear on the specific issue in question. Thus we affirm the fourth answer: faith is the presupposition of revelation, but revelation transforms and perfects faith.

This answer, however, leaves one question up in the air, namely, where does the original faith come from and what is its relation to revelation? An answer to this question is implied in the Bible and was drawn out at various points in the tradition, and especially in the moderate forms of neo-Reformation theology mentioned above. It is an answer which in its modern form makes use of the doctrine of general or universal revelation. This answer is that general revelation is the presupposition of faith in a rudimentary form which is then the presupposition of special revelation. Let us explore the grounds for this answer.

Throughout the Bible and the tradition it is affirmed that God's glory is manifest in the creation (Ps. 19:1-4), that all people stand in relation to

God, that God is present to all people as creator, judge, and savior. All nations stand under the grace and judgment of God who is the Lord of all humanitiy (Amos 9:7). Also all people stand in a covenant relation to God. In the covenant with Noah and his descendants God promises the divine favor as manifested in the order of nature (Gen. 9:1-17). Jesus often praises the faith and love of gentiles (Mt. 8:5-13, Lk. 17:11-19). Paul argues that pagans are responsible for their idolatry, because they should have known God through the revelation in the creation and because God's law is written on their hearts (Rom. 1:19-20, 2:14-15). A similar view is put into the mouth of Paul in the Book of Acts. Here Paul asserts that God has never been without a witness among the gentiles, that God's goodness has been shown forth in the gifts of the creation, and that God is not far from anyone (Acts 14:15-17, 17:22-31). In the prologue to the Fourth Gospel it is asserted that the word who is God's agent in the creation of the world is the light which enlightens all people (Jn. 1:1-5, 9).

The apologists used this passage to argue that since all people participate in the word or logos, the more they conform their lives to the logos the closer they are to being Christians, and that therefore the greater pagans are in fact Christians.[2] They also claimed that God used pagan philosophy as a preparation for the gospel.[3] Calvin argued on the basis of Paul that God has planted in all people a sense of the divine or a seed of religion, and that God is revealed in the glory of creation and in the experience of humanity.[4] The moderate neo-Reformation theologians mentioned above developed the idea of general or universal revelation to mean that various elements in human experience can be interpreted as manifestations of and responses to the presence of God. Thus conscience, moral commitment, dedication to truth, justice, and beauty, devotion to the divine, and the experience of hope, love, joy, and peace are seen as responses to general revelation and as rudimentary forms of faith. These ideas have been elaborated in a different way by modern Roman Catholic authors, such as Karl Rahner in his concepts of the supernatural existential, anonymous Christianity, and implicit faith, and in the documents of Vatican II.

The grounds for this fifth answer seem to be weighty enough to cause us to combine it with our fourth answer. This is possible because they are complementary. Thus our final answer takes the following form: General revelation is the presupposition of faith in a rudimentary form, which is then the presupposition of special revelation, which in turn transforms and perfects this rudimentary faith.

Comment: It would, of course, have been possible to list this fifth answer among the original possible answers and include the grounds for it with the original exploration of the Bible and the tradition. However, I chose to leave it in the form given in order to indicate the way in which an insight can be gained in working on a question.

3

Authority

Should experience be the main criterion of theology?

This question is near the center of theological debate today. In reaction
to the liberal theology of the nineteenth and early twentieth centuries the
neo-orthodox theology of the second quarter of this century rejected experience as the main criterion of theology in favor of the authority of the
Bible. Then the secular and radical theology of the third quarter of this
century alleged the breakdown of neo-orthodoxy and the authority of the
Bible and appealed again to experience as the criterion of theology.[1] Now
various liberation theologies appeal to the experience of the oppressed,
blacks, women, gays, and third world people, as the criterion of theology.
Also romantic counter-cultural theologies appeal to various types of experience, bodily experience, the experience of play, drugs, meditation, the
collective unconscious, and so forth, as the criterion of theology.[2] There is
a hunger for experience in our culture generally and in the Christian
church and theology in particular. So the question inquires about a fairly
common and widely debated theological thesis of the latter half of this
century. Furthermore, it is also an important existential question for many
Christians today. Does my religious experience fit with my understanding
of Christian faith? Does my faith illuminate and make sense of my experience? If not, what does this mean for my faith?

Now is this a theological question? It is not a question about God or
about the world in relation to God. It is, however, a question about
questions about God and the world in relation to God. It is a question
about theological questions, about the criterion for resolving them. Thus
it is an indirect or meta-theological question. Are meta-theological questions to be resolved in the same way as theological questions? It is difficult
to see how they could be resolved in any other way, since they have
important theological implications. Questions about the theological criterion are decisive for all other theological questions, since they determine
how they are to be resolved.

In a question about the theological criterion, however, the obvious
problem is that of the theological criterion by which it will be resolved.

Presupposing a criterion would be begging the question, but doing theology without a criterion is impossible. The only way to approach such a question is a circular one, namely, to inquire about which answer is most coherent with the general interpretation of Christian faith which is being affirmed by the one pursuing the question. When the criterion has been determined in this way, one's understanding of Christian faith must be critically examined in the light of it. Then the coherence of the criterion with this, perhaps, revised, understanding of Christian faith can be tested, and so forth, on the analogy of the method of successive approximations in mathematics.

This is the necessary circularity of the approach to this type of question in theology as well as in philosophy and the human sciences. It is a circularity which is not vicious but which is essential to their character. As Tillich says, "Every understanding of spiritual things (*Geisteswissenschaften*) is circular."[3] The reason for this is that the criterion of theology cannot be external or prior to Christian faith but must be internal to it. For every element of Christian theology including the criterion is dependent upon all the other elements.

Some of the terms of the question require clarification. As indicated above, we are interpreting "criterion of theology" to refer to that to which one appeals in assessing the validity of a theological proposal. The "main" criterion will be the most important or decisive one but not necessarily the only one.

"Experience" is a very vague term and it requires a great deal of specification as to its scope. It can refer to sense experience, inner experience, religious experience, or the totality of experience. It can refer to the experience of the individual, the group, or all of humanity. It can refer to current, remembered, or all of experience. Let us interpret the question to be referring to Christian religious experience. This, however, can be understood in a variety of ways. It can refer to particular occasions of heightened awareness, to the depth dimension of all experience, or to all of experience seen from a particular point of view. It can range from the current Christian religious experience of the person pursuing the question to the totality of religious experience in Christian history. Let us assume that it refers to experience which is focussed in the awareness of the presence of God but which includes all experience when seen in the light of the former. Since the theologians who affirm some form of this criterion usually refer to contemporary experience, let us assume that the question refers to current and remembered experience.

Finally, the determination of the limits of the term "Christian" is a complex issue, and some theologians who affirm this criterion have limited their purview to particular groups, for example, the oppressed. In an ecumenical age, however, it is appropriate to include all Christians who claim that name and whose faith is focussed in some way on Jesus Christ.

Now we can reformulate the question. Should the current and remembered religious experience of all Christians be the main criterion of theology? What are the possible answers to this question?

1. Yes. The current and remembered religious experience of all Christians should be the main criterion of theology.

2. No. It should not be the main criterion of theology nor any criterion at all.

3. It should be a criterion of theology but not the main one.

Our procedure will be to explore each possible answer in turn. Following the discussion above we shall proceed by assessing the possible grounds for each answer in the light of the interpretation of Christian faith which is affirmed by the author, that is, the one summarized in the text.

1. Yes. The current and remembered religious experience of all Christians should be the main criterion of theology. At all the crucial turning points of Christian history religious experience has been the main criterion of theology. It was the experience of the prophets and apostles in which the revelation of God was received. The Bible is the record of this experience and its interpretation as the experience of the presence of God in self-disclosure, judgment, and salvation.

Jacob saw a vision of God in a dream and heard the Lord speaking to him at Bethel. Moses saw the burning bush and heard the Lord reveal his name and call him to lead the people of Israel out of Egypt. Isaiah saw a vision of God in the temple and heard the divine word of forgiveness and the divine call to be a prophet. Peter had heard Jesus teaching and had seen him heal the sick. When Jesus asked him who he believed Jesus was, Peter suddenly experienced the realization that Jesus was the Messiah. On the road to Damascus Paul saw a bright light and heard the risen Christ speaking to him. He was converted and his life and the life of the church were changed by this experience. In the Book of Acts it is often recorded that people heard the preaching of the apostles, experienced the presence of the Holy Spirit, and became Christians. In all these cases it was the experience which was decisive. So any appeal to the Bible is an appeal to religious experience.

Religious experience has also been decisive in the tradition of the church. Although most Christian authors appealed to the Bible, it was their own experience that was more important. A good example is the formation of the New Testament canon. The reasons given for canonicity of the New Testament books at various times were authorship by an apostle or an associate of an apostle, accordance with the consensus of received doctrine, wide usage in the church, address to the whole church, a unified message, and antiquity. These, however, were rationalizations after the fact. In reality the churches of the second and third centuries knew which books they wanted in the New Testament on the basis of their experience. They were the ones which testified to the love of God in Christ with such authenticity and power that they converted people, drew them into the church, and produced the fruit of the Spirit in the community. Thus the selection of the books of the New Testament canon was on the basis of contemporary Christian religious experience.

Another example is the Arian controversy. Arius had proposed an interpretation of Christ as an intermediary being between God and humanity, a creature who was neither divine nor human. However, the testimony of the contemporary Christian experience of salvation was that it was the God who had created them who saved them in Christ. So Athanasius argued against Arius that it was God who was present in Christ to save. Thus Arius' teaching was rejected because it was found to be incoherent with Christian experience. To be sure Athanasius appealed to the New Testament in confuting Arius, but as we have seen this was an appeal to the record and interpretation of earlier Christian experience.

Similar examples can be given from the later Christian tradition. For example, Augustine argued against Pelagius' view of sin and grace on the basis of his Christian experience of conversion and salvation. Luther protested against the late medieval practice of indulgences, because his Christian experience was that salvation was by grace and not by works. Calvin held to the authority of the Bible in theology, but he affirmed that the Bible is known as the word of God for the church and the individual Christian only through the inner testimony of the Holy Spirit. Thus it was the experience of the presence of God the Holy Spirit which was the supreme authority for Calvin. Finally, in the last century Schleiermacher, the father of modern theology, held that Christian theology is simply an account of the Christian religious affections, feeling, or consciousness.

So today the main criterion of our theological judgments should be our own Christian experience and that of our fellow Christians in so far as this is available to us. Thus our theology is confirmed or disconfirmed by our experience of our life before God. Tillich calls this experiential verification.[4]

2. No. The current and remembered Christian religious experience of all Christians should not be the main criterion of theology nor any criterion at all. Experience has very rarely been the criterion of theology, and when it has been, it has usually led theology astray. The reason for this can be seen clearly in the Bible. According to the prophets the religious experience of the people of Israel was riddled with idolatry, unfaithfulness, pagan superstition, spiritual blindness and perversity, hypocrisy, injustice, and immorality (Amos 2: 6-8, Isa. 1:1-17, Jer. 5:20-31, 7:8-11). As soon as God made a covenant with the people of Israel they were found worshipping the golden calf (Ex. 32). Their worship was corrupt; the prophets prophesied falsely as the people desired; the priesthood was venal (Amos 5:21-27, Isa. 1:11-15, 2:8, 30:8-14, Jer. 2:4-13). The only way this was overcome was by the power of the divine word spoken through the few

true prophets and by the Lord of history overthrowing and disproving the words of the false prophets and judging sinful Israel.

In the New Testament the religious experience of the disciples of Jesus was apparently hopelessly confused and obscure. Jesus often despaired of breaking through their darkness of mind and hardness of heart and quoted the prophets to them. "Do you not yet perceive or understand? Are your hearts hardened? Having eyes do you not see, and having ears do you not hear? And do you not remember?" (Mk. 8:17-18; see Isa. 6:9-10, Jer. 5:21). According to Matthew Jesus interprets Peter's sudden realization that he is the Christ as the result of divine revelation. However, Peter immediately misunderstands this so badly that Jesus describes him, the first of the apostles, as satan, as a hindrance to him, and on the side of humanity rather than God (Mt. 16:23). Later Peter denies Jesus three times. In the end the religious experience of the disciples was such that they all forsook Jesus and fled. It was not their religious experience with Jesus that brought them to Christian faith, but rather it was the powerful manifestation of the risen Christ which overcame their spiritual blindness and deafness and converted them. Finally, Paul had many intense and unusual Christian religious experiences, but he never appeals to them but rather to his weakness and thus to the power of Christ (2 Cor. 12:1-10). So one cannot appeal to the Bible to support the idea that religious experience should be the criterion of theology.[5]

The same applies to the tradition of the church. Besides being deeply influenced by unconscious forces and social pressures, Christian religious experience has always been distorted by sin, by estrangement from and rebellion against God. Calvin describes human nature as "a perpetual factory of idols."[6] Thus Christian experience has assumed a great variety of forms in Christian history: docetic, gnostic, arian, montanist, pelagian, catharist, spiritualist, rationalist, deist, romantic, and fascist, not to mention racist and sexist. Barth characterizes all religion and religious experience, including Christian, as unbelief, that which contradicts revelation.[7] His argument is one-sided and exaggerated but essentially correct. This great variety and instability makes Christian religious experience useless as a criterion of theology.

As Tillich states, our faith is confirmed or disconfirmed in our life experience before God. This applies, however, to our Christian faith as a whole and also to our life experience over the long run. It does not apply to specific theological proposals or to the brief period in which a person might be assessing a proposal. Furthermore, much of Christian religious experience would be found to be irrelevant to many theological proposals, either neutral, neither confirming nor disconfirming them, or capable of being interpreted either way.

Philosophers have noted that Christian faith is unusually impervious to experience. Antony Flew argues that theological assertions when pressed by the facts of experience often die a "death by a thousand qualifications."

> Someone tells us that God loves us as a father loves his children. We are reassured. But then we see a child dying of inoperable cancer of the throat. His earthly father is driven frantic in his efforts to help, but his Heavenly Father reveals no obvious sign of concern. Some qualification is made—God's love is "not a merely human love" or it is "an inscrutable love." . . . But then perhaps we ask: what is this assurance of God's (appropriately qualified) love worth? . . . Just what would have to happen . . . to entitle us to say "God does not love us"?[8]

In the long run it may sometimes be the case that repeated experience of natural will lead a person to deny the goodness or love of God. As noted above, however, this is over the long run and applies to one's whole Christian faith rather than to a particular theological proposal. The goodness or love of God is so fundamental a Christian assertion that denial of it would amount to denial of Christian faith as a whole.

Another problem with religious experience as a theological criterion is the accessibility of the "current and remembered Christian religious experience of all Christians." The experience of the individual inquirer is available only through the most careful and painstaking introspection and reflection. The gathering of similar data on a scientific sample in one congregation would constitute a very extensive research project. For a whole denomination, let alone all denominations in a nation or in all nations, it would obviously be far beyond any possibility of accomplishment.

A further difficulty in the appeal to religious experience is constituted by the fact that without the proper concepts a subject matter apparently cannot be experienced at all. "Nothing is ever experienced unless it is experienced *as* something; and if the conception in terms of which the thing is to be experienced is impossible [or unknown] to us, the experience itself is impossible."[9] Or as Anselm has put it, "He who will not believe will not gain experience."[10] So it seems that experience must appeal to concepts which are affirmed in order to be validated rather than the other way around. To the degree that this is true, any appeal to experience will always tend to validate the concepts (or theological affirmations) being used to interpret (and thus make possible) the experience. In simpler terms this means that religious experience will usually tend to confirm preexisting theological concepts and thus will not be an important criterion for theology.

A final difficulty in the appeal to religious experience to assess theological proposals is the one indicated by Tillich. Christian religious experience in order to function as a theological criterion must involve the use of a prior criterion to distinguish religious experience from the rest of experience, Christian religious experience from the rest of religious experience, and authentic Christian religious experience from the rest of Christian experience. In the nature of the case this criterion and its validity cannot be derived from the experience but must be bought to it. Then this criterion functions as the theological criterion and the experience itself does not. Thus as P. T. Forsyth has put it, "Nothing can be an authority for us which is not experienced, but the experience is not the authority." Or as Tillich has stated, "Experience is not the source from which the contents of systematic theology are taken, but the medium through which they are existentially received."[11]

3. The current and remembered Christian religious experience of all Christians should be a criterion of theology but not the main one. Both of the first two answers are one-sided but contain some truth. This answer suggests that these elements of truth can be combined in a coherent way. It suggests that Christian experience, especially that of the inquirer and those whose experience is accessible to the inquirer, should play some part in the assessment of theological proposals, but that it cannot function as the main criterion. In order to specify this part more clearly we need to gain a more accurate picture of the relation between experience and theology.

What are the possible relations between some particular segment of Christian religious experience and a particular theological proposal? The closest possible relation can be called complementarity. This means that there is a good fit or coherence between them. On the one hand, this means that the proposal orders, makes sense of, illuminates, and gives meaning to the experience and thus successfully interprets it. On the other hand, it means that the experience confirms, supports, or gives evidence for the proposal. These are the two aspects of complementarity.

The next possible relation between some Christian religious experience and a theological proposal is that of independence. This would mean that there was no significant relation between the two or a lack of complementarity. The proposal does not make sense of the experience, and the experience does not support or confirm the proposal. The experience implies nothing one way or the other about the proposal.

A third possible relation between a religious experience and a theological proposal is that of contradiction or incoherence. This is not simply a lack of complementarity or independence but a negative relation. On the one hand, the proposal not only fails to illuminate and make sense of the experience, but somehow contradicts it. On the other hand, the experience not only does not support, confirm, or give evidence for the proposal but in fact undercuts, disconfirms, or gives evidence against the proposal, perhaps by implying a contradictory proposal.

Thus there will be a spectrum of possible relations between a segment of Christian religious experience and a particular theological proposal. The principle of this spectrum will be the degree of complementarity, and it will move from complete complementarity through independence to contradiction. Then experience will function as a criterion of a proposal by manifesting a certain degree of complementarity on such a spectrum.

A further complication of the relation between experience and theology is that we can expect to find that the relation of some theological affirmations to experience is closer than others. We may expect to find, for example, that theological proposals in the areas of sin, grace, and salvation are more closely related to experience than those in the areas of trinity and eschatology. Thus various theological topics could be placed on a second spectrum whose principle is the closeness of relation to experience. This principle may also be the relative directness with which the topics deal with the relation of God to humanity. Certain topics deal more with God in distinction from the creation, while others deal more with God's relation to the creation. However, since God is one, it will be the case that the former will have their echo in Christian religious experience and thus will to some extent be accessible through it. In any case experience will be more informative about some theological proposals than others.

Therefore, Christian religious experience can be used as a criterion in theology subordinate to scripture and tradition. It can function to confirm or question theological proposals grounded on these authorities. A common situation in theology is that of judging between alternative proposals. When the appeal to scripture and tradition is equally well grounded for two proposals, then that proposal is to be favored which is more complementary with Christian experience, that is, which orders, makes sense of, gives meaning to, and thus interprets the experience more successfully than the other. Of course, the wider the sample of Christian experience investigated, the more weight it would carry. On the other hand, the experience must be tested by scripture and tradition to discern its spirit (1 Cor. 12:10, 1 Jn. 4:1).[12] A situation of contradiction between Christian experience and a theological proposal should be the occasion for such testing and also for reassessing the basis of the proposal.

I conclude that the third answer is the most coherent with the general interpretation of Christian faith which is being affirmed.

Comment: In this chapter (and in some others) in elaborating the possible answers I have employed an advocacy of rhetorical style. In other chapters I have tried to give a balanced case for each possible answer. The reason is that on the question addressed in this chapter the answers and the supporting arguments are complex and subtle and thus can be brought out and distinguished more easily by a more adversarial style.

4

Trinity

Is it necessary to believe in the doctrine of the trinity in order to be a Christian?

This question raises the fundamental issues of the relation of faith and doctrine and of what it is essentially to be a Christian. It is commonly held that faith means believing doctrines about God and the world. It is also often asserted that being a Christian means believing in certain fundamental doctrines such as the incarnation and the trinity. But does faith mean believing doctrines? And are there certain fundamental doctrines which must be believed if one is to be counted a Christian?

Several aspects of this question need clarification. First, the term "necessary" can have several meanings. It can mean logically necessary or implied in the ideas of being a Christian. It can mean morally necessary or required by Christian moral principles. It can mean legally necessary in the sense of being required by church discipline or canon law. It can mean theologically necessary. One way to clarify this is to ask, What kind of contradiction would it be, if any, to be a Christian and not to believe in the doctrine of the trinity? Would it be a logical, moral, canonical, or theological contradiction? If it is interpreted to be a canonical contradiction, then the question becomes one of church discipline rather than theology. Therefore, for this to be a theological question, "necessary" must be interpreted to mean theologically necessary, that is, necessary in the light of the theological meaning of being a Christian. This is one interpretation of the meaning of logically necessary.

Secondly, there is the issue of the relation of faith or belief to doctrine. What does it mean to believe in a doctrine? Let us assume that a doctrine is a theological proposition about God or the world in relation to God. Believing in a doctrine could mean trusting in it as the source of meaning or fulfillment in life. It could mean assent to it on the basis of the authority of the church. It could mean to affirm that it is a true or accurate description of the way things are or a valid articulation of some aspect of Christian faith.

"Believing in" is often distinguished from "believing that." This distinction derives in part from the fact that English has no verb for the act of faith except "believe" and that "believe" has an intellectual connotation. One believes *in* a friend when one trusts the friend deeply. One believes *that* a friend's curriculum vitae is an accurate description of certain aspects of the friend's life. Thus one issue raised by the question is whether or not believing in a doctrine is an appropriate stance for a Christian. I would argue on the basis of the understanding of faith in the Bible that the object of faith is always God or God's action in Christ and not doctrines about this. One does not believe in a doctrine in the sense of trusting in it. Rather one believes that it is a valid articulation of some aspect of Christian faith or the Christian relation to God. Therefore, if the question is interpreted to mean trusting in the doctrine of the trinity, the answer must be negative. In order to continue with the question, let us interpret it to mean believing or judging that the doctrine of the trinity is a valid articulation of the Christian relation to God.

Thirdly, the question refers to *the* doctrine of the trinity and thus may imply that there is only one such doctrine or at least only one officially accepted doctrine. However, our survey of the history of the doctrine in the text has indicated that there are several doctrines of the trinity: Eastern, Western, social analogy, modal, and so forth. There is one doctrine in the sense of the threefold name of God of the rule of faith as found, for example, in the Apostles' Creed. This, however, is not yet a doctrine. It is ambiguous and can be interpreted in a number of ways. There is one doctrine in the sense of the Western formula of "three persons in one substance." However, this formula is also ambiguous if not misleading and can be interpreted in a number of ways. A doctrine of the trinity would presumably be one interpretation of this formula. So the question can be interpreted to refer to any of a number of widely accepted interpretations of the threefold confession of the rule of faith or to one particular interpretation of this confession. Since the answer to the question would obviously be negative if we chose the latter alternative, let us assume that the phrase "the doctrine of the trinity" in the question refers to any of a number of widely accepted interpretations of the threefold name of God in the role of faith.

Finally, there is the question of what it means to be a Christian. This is obviously the decisive issue in the question. It can be and has been resolved in a number of ways in Christian history. It can be treated in terms of minimum essentials, in which case the answer would probably be negative, or in terms of the fullness of being a Christian, in which case the answer might be positive. It can focus on being a member of the church or on the Christian relation to God, on the "outward and visible" or on the "inward and spiritual." The definition of what is required for membership in the church will vary from church to church. However, to resolve the issue by reference to some particular church would turn the question into one of church discipline or canon law. So we must aim at a theological definition of what it means to be a Christian.

I would argue on the basis of the Bible and the tradition that being a Christian is identical with being a member of the church, and that this involves a confession of faith in the threefold form of the rule of faith, such as the Apostles' Creed, baptism in the threefold name of God, and participation in the eucharist. This is the outward and visible aspect. I would also argue that the Christian relation to God is essentially trust in, love of, communion with, and obedience to God as creator and redeemer, and that this relation is properly articulated in the threefold confession of faith in God as Father, Son, and Holy Spirit.

With these clarifications and interpretations the question can be rephrased as follows: Is it theologically necessary in order to be a Christian to believe that any of the widely accepted interpretations of the threefold name of God in a doctrine of the trinity is a valid articulation of the Christian relation to God? The possible answers to this question are obviously Yes and No. I will argue for a negative answer.

I have stated that being a Christian means making the threefold confession of faith and being baptized in the threefold name of God. The importance of this threefold confession and baptism is that it is an account of the new situation into which the believer is brought through baptism. It indicates the structure or pattern of the Christian's relation to God. God the Father brings the Christian into communion with God by the divine action in Christ and through the working of God the Holy Spirit (see, for example, Tit. 3:5–7).

The making of this confession and the acceptance of baptism in this threefold name involves the faith that God has saved us through Christ and that we participate in this through the Holy Spirit. It also involves the belief that this faith can be articulated and explicated in a way which is intelligible, consistent, and coherent. The reason for this is that the consensus of the Bible as interpreted in the tradition is that God and God's relation to the world are rational, not in the superficial sense of technical reason but in the deeper sense of being intelligible and having order and meaning. Christian faith is a response to the word of God in the mouths of prophets and apostles and the word made flesh in Jesus Christ, and the word is the mode of communication between rational beings.

However, the confession of faith and the acceptance of baptism in the threefold name of God does not require the belief that any of the theories about the relations of the three names which were developed from the second century on is a valid articulation of the Christian's relation to God. They may all be, but that is probably not the case since some are contradictory. It may be that none of them is, but that would be highly unlikely. I believe that at least one is, but that belief is not theologically necessary for being a Christian.

5

God

Can God be both personal and infinite?

This question goes to the heart of the Christian understanding of God. There are strong grounds in Christian faith for affirming both the personhood and the infinity of God, but these two concepts seem to be contradictory. A good case can be made for affirming both that God stands in a personal relation with humanity and the world and also that God is not limited by space and time nor in power and goodness. The problem is that the only personal reality we know, namely human being, is essentially finite, bounded by space and time and limited in power and goodness. Thus it is difficult to see how there can be an infinite personal reality. So the importance of the question is that it points to an apparent contradiction in the Christian doctrine of God. I interpret the question to be asking whether or not we can affirm both personhood and infinity of God.

Since the question hangs on how we understand the concepts of personhood and infinity, we need some working definitions. Let us define "personal" as that quality which involves self-knowledge or self-transcendence, the quality implied by such human capacities as freedom, responsibility, love, and intentional action. Let us define "infinite" as the quality of being unlimited by anything external, that is, being only self-limited, in regard to space, time, and power. This means that what is infinite transcends space and time, and in the case of God it means that God comprehends and is present in all space and time. The concept of infinity is sometimes also interpreted to include the quality of being unlimited in goodness and love. We shall limit our attention to the former meaning, however, since finitude in space, time, and power is essential to humanity while finitude in goodness and love is not. This is indicated by the fact that Jesus is usually understood to be characterized by unlimited goodness and love, but not by infinity in regard to space, time, and power.

Now what would count as an answer to this question? There are two possible answers, the first of which has three forms.

1. No. God cannot be both personal and infinite.
   a. God is neither personal nor infinite.

    b. God is personal but not infinite.

    c. God is infinite but not personal.

  2. Yes. God can be both personal and infinite.

Let us consider these answers in order. Since, as I shall argue below, there are strong grounds for affirming that God is both personal and infinite, and since the negations of answer 1a. are included in answers 1b. and 1c., we can pass over answer 1a.

Answer 1b. has often been argued. Every argument that God is personal can be interpreted also as an argument that God is finite, since the only personal reality we know of first hand is finite. Furthermore, it has been argued in the light of the problem of evil that if we have to choose between the goodness and the omnipotence of God, we would have to choose the divine goodness and settle for a God of finite power.[1] This answer, however, must be weighed against the arguments that God is infinite.

Although infinity is not a biblical concept, its various meanings are implied about God throughout the Bible. God is infinite in the sense of being present in every place and every time (Ps. 90:2, 4; Ps. 139:7-12). God is infinite in the sense of being unlimited in power and knowledge (Ps. 147:5, Job 38-41, Isa. 51:6). God is infinite in the sense of transcending space and time and is thus called eternal (Deut. 33:27, Isa. 40:8, Rom. 1:20, 1 Tim. 1:17, 1 Pet. 5:10). Moreover, the theological tradition is unanimous in affirming the infinite character of God. Therefore, I conclude that answer 1b. is incorrect.

In regard to answer 1c. we need to assess the arguments for the personal character of God. It is rarely if ever argued that God is sub-personal, but it is often claimed that God is supra-personal. What does it mean to say that God is supra-personal? It could mean in the highest or eminent sense personal. Would this make God's personhood any more coherent with God's infinity? Since the concept of the supra-personal is vague, it is not clear whether or not it involves finitude. This will be explored further below. On the other hand, if "supra-personal" means something beyond personal, then it may come down to something sub-personal, since the personal is the highest concept we know.[2] Of course, the mysterious reality of God is beyond the personal in the sense of being beyond human personal reality as we know it in ourselves.

Although "personal" is not a biblical concept, it is the universal consensus of the authors of the Bible that God is to be understood as personal. God's relation to humanity and the creation is described almost exclusively in anthropomorphic terms. This is emphasized in the widespread reference to the name and face of God, and it culminates in the New Testament consensus that God is fully revealed in Jesus Christ.[3]

The theological tradition did not explicitly affirm the personhood of God in the early centuries, because the influence of Greek philosophy on the development of the doctrine of the trinity produced a concept of "person" which was quite different from the modern concept and which could not be attributed to the unity of God. The personhood of God in the modern sense was not affirmed until the eighteenth century when the modern concept of person began to be developed.[4] However, the personal character of God in the modern sense was implied in most of the tradition and has been almost universally affirmed since the eighteenth century.

Therefore, I conclude that we must affirm that God is personal, and that answer 1c. is invalid.

This leaves answer 2 to be investigated. If we discover that this solution to the question is not viable, then we still have to conclude that the Christian doctrine of God is fundamentally incoherent. Can the concepts "personal" and "infinite" be understood in a way which is non-contradictory and coherent? Can we conceive of a personal reality which is infinite in the sense of being unlimited by anything external, being only self-limited in regard to space, time, and power, and thus transcending space and time in the sense of being present at all points in space and time?

In the development of human personality toward maturity we can see the beginnings of the transcending of time in memory and anticipation.[5] We can see intimations of the transcending of space in the imaginative and sympathetic participation in the situation of other persons, places, and things. We can see suggestions of the transcending of finitude in knowledge in increasing self-awareness and understanding of the world. And we can see the beginnings of the transcending of finite power in the increasing capacity for the exercise of all the functions of the person, also as extended by modern technology. Tillich interprets sanctification in terms of increasing awareness, freedom, relatedness, and transcendence.[6]

Let us consider the analogy of the early British monarchy. It was centered in the personal reality of the monarch and was present in all places in the realm by means of representatives and structures such as magistrates, courts, and laws. Such representatives and structures bore the full authority of the monarchy in maintaining order and in dispensing justice and mercy. The monarchy was not finite in time, the succession being automatic. The limitations of this analogy are obvious. There is no eternal transcending of space and time, and the exercise of the power of the monarch is indirect. But the analogy indicates that the concepts of personhood and infinity may not be incoherent.

The English philosopher John Macmurray argued not only that the concepts of personality and infinity or universality are coherent but also that they are necessary to each other. (He uses infinity and universality interchangeably.) In personal unity as against mathematical and organic unity individuality and universality are not contradictory but reciprocal. The hallmark of personality is self-transcendence, our capacity to comprehend the universe, to enter sympathetically into the life of nature and other persons, to represent and act for others.

> The wider the range and the deeper the penetration of our interests, the more human, the more individual, the more personal we become. In a word, the more universal a person becomes in his self-transcendence, the more unique does he become in his individuality. There is therefore no ground for hesitation in ascribing personality to God. Absolute personality, in terms of our analysis, must involve absolute universality and absolute individuality at once, each of these qualities being the condition of the other.[7]

Charles Hartshorne has put this somewhat differently:

> A supreme person must be inclusive of all reality. We find that persons contain relations of knowledge and love to other persons and things, and since relations contain their terms, persons must contain other persons and things. If it seems otherwise, this is because of the inadequacy of human personal relations, which is such that the terms are not conspicuously and clearly contained in their subjects. To transfer to the adequately related subject [God] this apparent externality of terms is the opposite of judicious, however often it has been done in the past and is done now. In God, terms of his knowledge would be absolutely manifest and clear and not at all "outside" the knowledge of the knower.[8]

This analogy and hypothesis of the coherence of personality and universality or infinity can be tested in the case of Jesus Christ, who according to Christian faith is both infinite and personal.

Christian faith holds that in Jesus Christ we have the full and definitive self-disclosure of God. So in relation to Christ our question becomes, Can Christ be both infinite and personal? There would seem to be no problem in understanding Christ to be personal. But according to the tradition, his human personhood is not identical with the divine personhood. In the text, however, I argue that the best way to interpret the divinity of Christ is to state that the personal actions and functions of Jesus, especially in love, judgment, forgiveness, and healing, are numerically identical with God's actions and functions. In these actions of the personhood of Jesus we can see the actions of the personhood of God. In this sense the personhood of Christ is identical with the personhood of God.

In what sense can we understand Jesus Christ to be infinite or universal? His humanity was finite, but it was also universal in the sense indicated by Macmurray above. In a unique and ultimate degree Christ comprehended God and the world, entered sympathetically into the life of the creation, human beings, and history, and acted on behalf of all people.

In the language of the Fourth Gospel and the tradition Jesus Christ was the incarnation of the divine logos, the universal principle ordering all reality, the creative word or reason of God. Tillich describes the logos doctrine of Christ as "the identity of the absolutely concrete with the absolutely universal."[9]

To be sure, Jesus in his human life and ministry was finite, limited in space and time and power and thus not infinite. But Christian faith affirms that the risen Christ is present in all times and places by the Spirit of Christ, the Holy Spirit of God, and this is infinite in the proper theological sense. So I conclude that the hypothesis of the coherence of the divine infinity or universality and the divine personhood is confirmed in Jesus Christ.

This thesis of the coherence of personhood and infinity can be analyzed and elaborated conceptually in various ways. Tillich has proposed one way. All of reality is informed by a polarity of two principles, individualization and participation (among others). Since God is the source and ground of all reality, each of these principles can and must be attributed to God analogically. Attributing individuality to God means that God is personal. Attributing participation to God means that God is present in and to all of reality, in all times and spaces. But because God is the ground of reality, God transcends this polarity and these two principles are perfectly united in God in a way which we cannot easily conceive.[10]

Therefore, I conclude that the relevant meaning of the concepts of personal and infinite are not contradictory but coherent, and that the second answer is the correct one.

6

Creation

What is the relation between the statements, "God created me," and "My parents produced me"?

This question might arise for people who wonder what it means to be a creature of God when they know very well how they came into being biologically and that this process apparently has nothing to do with God and seems perfectly intelligible apart from God. They may have in mind and phrase from the old Anglican catechism, "God the Father, who hath made me and all the world." Is this just a poetic or mythological way of describing the biological process of human reproduction, or is it saying something more? Is it just a pious way of referring to the individual's place in a universe which has its ultimate origin in God, or is it referring to a more direct relation between the action of God and the origin of the individual?

Let us assume that creation means that God is the ultimate origin and sustainer of the universe, including the individual person, and that therefore everything is absolutely dependent upon God for its origin and continued existence, including the individual person. Let us also assume that "produced" refers to the organic process of human reproduction as understood by biology. Now since an individual person did not exist at the beginning but came into existence relatively recently, "God created me" implies that God had something to do with my coming into being when I did besides being the ultimate origin of the universe and its various processes. It implies some kind of active decision on God's part. Also human reproduction implies a decision and action upon the part of the parents. So one aspect of the question is whether or not it is possible to conceive of two distinct actions being the cause of an identical result, namely, the emergence of an individual person.

I interpret the question to be asking about the relation of theological and biological statements about the origin of the individual person. There are seven types of logical relations between statements.[1] Of these four are relevant to this question: equivalence, contradiction, independence, and complementarity, which is logically a form of independence. These are the possible answers to the question, and they can be outlined as follows:

1. The statements are equivalent. This means that they are either both true or both false. This would be the case if the first were simply a mythological or poetic version of the second or were identical with the second.

2. The statements are contradictory. This means that when one is true the other is false. This would be the case if the statements were mutually exclusive, for example, in the sense that one and only one agency could be said to be the cause of the emergence of the individual person.

3. The statements are independent. This means that the truth or falsity of one statement does not affect the truth or falsity of the other. It can also mean that the statements have no significant relation. This would be the case if the statements were interpreted to be saying quite different things about the origin of the individual.

4. The statements are complementary. This means that the statements are logically independent but do in fact have a significant relation, namely, that they describe different aspects of one reality.

Our procedure will be to investigate each possible answer in turn.

1. The statements are equivalent. We have defined creation as the affirmation that God is the ultimate origin and sustainer of the universe including every person. The biological understanding of human reproduction refers to the specific organic process by which conception and the growth of the fertilized egg takes place. These concepts of ultimate origin and sustainer and of biological process are quite distinct.

However, the concept of ultimate origin means more than the origin behind or before all proximate origins. The idea that God created the universe at the beginning, set it going according to the laws of nature, and then retired from the scene, so to speak, has usually been rejected in the tradition as deism. The Bible and the tradition have generally taught the continuing creation of the universe by God in the sense not only of sustaining and preserving but also of the bringing into being of the new (Ps. 104:14, 30, 139:13, 147:8). This brings the concepts somewhat closer together, but they remain distinct.

Furthermore, the statement "God created me" when made by a Christian amounts to a confession of faith that one owes one's existence to God, a confession of dependence upon God, an expression of thanksgiving to God, and a commitment to obedience to God. It expresses a particular orientation toward God and the world, seeing the world as a gift of God to which the attitude of stewardship is the appropriate response. No doubt something analogous to this is expressed in the statement "My parents produced me." However, these statements remain distinct; one can be affirmed without the other.

Thus creation and reproduction are two distinct ways of looking at the emergence of the individual person, and neither can be reduced to the other. Therefore, the statements are not equivalent.

2. The statements are contradictory. The two statements would be contradictory if they referred to one identical process and if there could be only one agency which was the cause of the process. The two statements do in fact refer to one identical process, namely, the emergence of the individual person out of the union of the parents. Are the two agencies, God and the parents, to be considered mutually exclusive alternatives as the cause of the process? They were not so understood in the Bible which asserts the activity both of the parents and God in the emergence of the individual. God says to Abraham in regard to Sarah, "I will give you a son by her" (Gen. 17:16; see 21:1-2, 25:21, 30:22-23). Job says to God, "Thy hands fashioned and made me" (Job 10:8; see Ps. 139:13-16, Jer. 1:5). These assertions about the activity of God do not deny but rather assume the activity of the parents in the origin of the individual.

The same is true of the tradition of the church, although there was some confusion on this particular issue. On the one hand, Tertullian, Gregory of Nyssa, and probably Augustine taught traducianism, the view that each soul is derived from the parents along with the body. The whole person is produced by the generative act of the parents but is also the creation of God. On the other hand, Cyril of Alexandria, Lactantius, Ambrose, and Jerome taught creationism, the view that each individual soul was created independently by God at the moment of its infusion into the body at conception. The body was understood to be derived from the parents, although it was still seen as the creation of God. The issue was not whether God created both body and soul, but rather whether God created the soul through propagation with the body or through a special act of creation.[2]

Creationism came to prevail in the catholic and Reformed traditions, and traducianism in the Lutheran tradition. Neither tradition, however, saw a contradiction between God's creation of the whole person and the natural process of human generation. Therefore there seem to be no grounds for asserting that the statements are contradictory.

3. The statements are independent. It is clear that the statements in the question are logically independent. The truth or falsity of one does not affect the truth or falsity of the other. However, they are not independent in the broader sense of having no significant relation to each other. The reason for this is that both statements refer to the same identical process, namely, the emergence of the individual person. This leads us directly to the next answer.

4. The statements are complementary. This means that the statements refer to different aspects of one reality. In investigating the second answer

we discovered that in both the Bible and the tradition both statements were made at the same time about the emergence of the individual. A person was understood to be created by God and produced by the parents at the same time. This in itself suggests that the statements are complementary. To be sure, in the tradition two different kinds of complementarity were involved. In the case of creationism there was joint agency only in regard to the body, whereas in traducianism the joint action included both body and soul.

However, can two distinct agencies be the cause of one identical result? Frank B. Dilley denies that this is possible. He states, "It is not possible to conceive of two sets of free causes operating conjointly in exactly the same action." "If there is genuine unity of action, two parties doing exactly the same act at the same time, then there is no duality of causes, and if there is duality of causes, then there is no unity of action."[3] Or as David R. Griffin puts it, "If 'sufficient' really means *sufficient*, then the idea of two sufficient causes for one event is clearly self-contradictory."[4]

This objection is correct when the causes in question are of the same kind, that is, finite, and are operating in the same manner or mode. However, it is not necessarily valid when one cause is finite and the other infinite, or when the causes are not operating in the same mode. Aristotle distinguished four kinds of causes: material, formal, efficient and final. Thomas Aquinas and Calvin used these distinctions to describe the coactivity of divine and creaturely causes, which they distinguished as primary or principal and secondary, proximate, contingent, or intermediate causes.[5]

Thomas takes up this specific objection: "The same work cannot proceed at the same time from two sources. . . . Therefore, if the creature's operation is from God operating in the creature, it cannot at the same time proceed from the creature; and so no creature works at all." Then after distinguishing three causes or principles of action, the end, the agent, and the form (he rejects matter as a cause), Thomas explains that God operates as a cause in three ways: as the end of every action, as the first cause of all agents, and as giving and preserving the forms and powers of all things. He concludes by replying to the above objection. "One action does not proceed from two agents of the same order. But nothing hinders the same action from proceeding from a primary agent and a secondary agent."[6]

Similarly Calvin, taking the example of the Chaldeans afflicting Job (Job 1:17), explains how the same work can be attributed to God, Satan, and the Chaldeans, distinguishing their actions in terms of their ends and their manner of acting.[7] This unity of the divine and the creaturely activity is a pattern throughout the Bible.[8] However, is this understanding of the coactivity of divine and finite agents in one identical action coherent with the modern scientific understanding of causation? Various attempts have been made to explain such coherence.[9] Perhaps the most successful is that informed by process philosophy.

In the terms of this philosophy God in the divine primordial nature acts in the world by presenting to each actual occasion or event the relevant eternal objects or possibilities for its prehension and also the initial aim or principle of concretion for its action. The divine consequent nature acts by being felt or prehended by each actual occasion in its action. On its own side each actual occasion prehends the relevent possibilities for its action, the initial aim presented by God, and the consequent nature of God. It also prehends the relevant past actual occasions and synthesizes all of these things into an occasion whose novelty derives from its own subjective aim.[10] To be sure in this analysis of the relation of divine and creaturely causes the two agencies can be said to produce the same overall result, but they contribute distinct elements to the process. Thus it cannot be said that the two agencies are the cause of an identical result at this level. The modern Thomistic interpretation of the relation of primary and secondary causes, however, makes this latter claim.

So I conclude that Dilley's and Griffin's objections do not stand and that the fourth answer is correct, that the relation of the statements "God created me" and "my parents produced me" is complementary. This means that the two statements refer to different aspects of the one reality of the emergence of the individual person. It should be noted that this answer is more coherent with traducianism than with creationism. The parents produce the whole person, body and soul, and the whole person is also created by God. Traducianism is probably also more coherent with the scientific picture of the emergence of the individual.[11]

7

Providence

Are all events equally providential?

This question focuses on a very difficult issue in the doctrine of providence. It arises for someone who wonders, for example, whether a death from illness is as providential as an unusual recovery from illness, whether the typhoon which kills thousands of people is as providential as the gentle rain which saves thousands from drought, or whether the doings of Adolf Eichmann are as providential as those of Mother Theresa. It raises the question of whether God acts more in some events than in others, whether God as Lord is really in control of events. This issue has troubled Christians from the beginning. A positive answer to the question raises serious problems about God's goodness and love in relation to evil, both moral and natural, since it implies that God is responsible for evil. A negative answer, on the other hand, raises serious questions about God's power, the divine lordship over history.

The question obviously hangs on the meaning of "providential." In ordinary secular usage when we say that some event is providential, we usually mean that it fits in with or promotes some human purpose. We say that it is providential that someone dropped in on a particular occasion, because this person was able to do something which furthered some purpose of ours. In this ordinary sense some events are obviously more providential than others.

The ordinary religious meaning of providence is God's loving care for the well-being of each person, a loving care which is effective in carrying out its purpose (see Mt. 6:24-34, 7:10-11, 10:29-31 par). The ordinary religious meaning of "providential" is an extension of its secular meaning. An event is considered to be providential if it seems to be a manifestation of God's purpose of caring for the well-being of a person. In this ordinary religious sense some events are obviously more providential that others.

Let us define providence as God's carrying out the divine will or love to bring the creation, and especially each person, to its fulfillment. Then the term "providential" will mean that quality of an event which refers to its participation in God's providence as defined. In order to simplify the question let us limit our consideration to God's providential care for human beings. This limitation also affects our definition of the term "events." Let us assume that "events" refers to all occurrences which have a significant bearing on the well-being of human beings.

Now should this question be interpreted to be an empirical or a conceptual one? That is, should it be interpreted to be inquiring whether all events can in fact be seen to be providential, or should it be interpreted to be inquiring about the meaning of the concept of providence? Of course, a solution to the former question may be contained in the latter. That is, it may be part of the concept of providence that all events can be seen to be providential. However, this is not generally the case in the Bible or the tradition. So let us assume that the question concerns the concept of providence and not its visibility.

Another aspect of the definition of providence needs clarification. The biblical and traditional term for fulfillment is salvation. Let us interpret fulfillment or salvation to mean the total well-being of the person, physical, psychological, social, and spiritual, which is based on the spiritual dimension, namely, the person's relationship to God, a relationship of trust, love, and communion. This fulfillment will always be partial or fragmentary in history and will be complete only in the final consummation. Then "providential" will mean that quality of an event which refers to its participation in the carrying out of the divine will to bring all persons to their fulfillment as defined. Any event which tends toward a person's total well-being will be providential, and any event which tends in the opposite direction will not be providential.

Since total well-being has several aspects or dimensions, physical, psychological, social, and spiritual, it may be that some events will be providential in promoting a person's well-being in one or more aspects but not in others. Should such an event be considered providential or not? Since a person's well-being is a unity, it would not be possible for one aspect to be significantly fulfilled or unfulfilled without affecting the fulfillment of the other aspects. Therefore, let us assume that an event which promotes a person's well-being directly in one or more aspects but not directly in others can be considered providential. Also an event may constitute the necessary basis of a person's existence and thus of the person's tending toward or away from fulfillment and yet be neutral in regard to the direction of such tending. Examples are the various biological processes of the human body. Such events can properly be considered to be indirectly providential.[1]

The interpretation of "equally" will probably be decisive in regard to the answer to the question. "Equal" can refer to equivalence in regard to measure, quality, mode, nature, or status. We have defined "providential" as a quality of participation in the process of the carrying out of the divine will. Equality of participation can refer to the measure, quality, mode, nature, or status of such participation. In this context I believe that in every case quality, nature, and status reduce to mode or measure. So we are left with these latter two.

It is quite clear that events differ in the mode of their participation in providence. They can participate inorganically (weather, geography, geology), organically (bodily processes, animals, plants), or humanly. It is also clear that events differ in the measure, degree, or importance of their participation in the process of providence. Physical and chemical actions and reactions participate less significantly in the process than human actions. Therefore if "equally" is interpreted to refer to the measure or mode of the participation of events in the process of providence, then the question will be answered in the negative by definition.

Now we are faced with a choice. We have resolved the original question through analysis. All events are not equally providential. We can stop here, or we can drop "equally" from the question and proceed with the new question, Are all events providential? Let us proceed. Now we can summarize our analysis and interpretation of the question by rephrasing it as follows: Do all events that have a significant bearing on human well-being participate in the carrying out of God's will to bring all people to their total well-being? The possible answers to this question are Yes and No. Our procedure will be to explore each of the possible answers in turn.

Yes. All events are providential. It is the unanimous testimony of the Bible and the theological tradition of the church that God is the lord of history, that God is in control of all events, and therefore God brings it about that all events serve the divine purpose of bringing the whole creation, and especially each person, to its fulfillment. As Paul says, "From God, and through God, and to God are all things" (Rom. 11:36). The main biblical image for this is the rule or kingship of God (Ex. 15:18, Ps. 47:7-8, Isa. 6:5, 1 Tim. 6:15). In the New Testament it is affirmed that this rule is exercised through Christ who is therefore known as king of kings (Rev. 17:14, 19:16). In particular God rules all events in nature for the welfare of all creatures (Job 38-41, Ps. 145:15-16, 147:9, Mt. 6:26, 30, 10:29), and especially each person (Mt. 6:25-33, 10:30, Rom. 8:28). God rules and controls human history, (Old Testament passim., Lk. 1:50-53, Acts 17:26-28, Rom. 11:30-32, 13:1-6, 1 Cor. 1:28-30) including every human action (Ps. 127:1, Prov. 16:1, 9, 19:21, 21:1, Isa. 26:12, 1 Cor. 12:6, Phil. 2:13). God even causes evil acts (Ex. 7:3, 1 Sam. 19:9, Ezek. 20:25-26, Isa. 6:9-10, 63:17, Mt. 13:13-15, Jn. 12:39-40, Acts 28:25-27, Rom. 9:18, 11:7-8, 2 Thess. 2:11-12). However, this is always a means to the fulfillment of the divine plan to bring the whole creation to its fulfillment. Thus God also overrules and uses natural and moral evil to fulfill the divine purposes (Gen. 45:5, 8, 50:20, Jn. 9:1-3, 11:4, Acts 2:23, 4:27-28).

Augustine elaborates these biblical themes regarding the sovereignty of God over all historical and natural events. God foreknows, controls, and acts in all events in order to fulfill the divine purpose for the creation.[2] According to Aquinas all things are subject to the government of God who rules everything immediately according to the design of providence and some things mediately according to the execution of this design through secondary causes. Thus God works in every action of every agent as its end, its first cause, and as its formal cause.[3] Calvin makes this view of the divine governance of all events even more rigorous. Every natural event and human action is decreed, willed, and directed by God.[4] D. M. Baillie summarizes this tradition as follows:

> Every Christian believes also that whatever comes to him comes from God, by God's appointment, God's providence. And not simply in the sense that God works through the natural (including the psychological) laws of His own ordaining; as if, having "wound up" the universe to run by these laws, He had then left it to run its course. The Christian believes that in some sense everything comes to him *directly* from God whose working is always individual.[5]

No. Not all events are providential. In creation there is a divine self-limitation. God gives time and space for the creatures, for their activity, spontaneity, limited autonomy, and relative freedom. The creatures are given powers and gifts which are to be used in their own development (Ps. 19:1-6, 104:14-26, 148:3-10). Humanity is given freedom and responsibility to people the earth and to rule over it (Gen. 1:28, Ps. 8:6). Thus creation sets in motion a real historical process which is not a sham or a divine puppet show. Otherwise God would be the sole agent in the creation. This would be a monism in which there is only one reality, God, and in which other things are simply aspects or attributes of this one reality (Spinoza). However, the view of the Bible and the tradition is that the creation is a reality distinct from God and with a relative independence of God. This is especially true of humanity whose freedom and responsibility are always affirmed. All this means that some events, especially in the human realm, may not participate in the carrying out of the divine will to bring all people to their fulfillment.

Assertions in the Bible that God acts directly in natural events and human actions are not to be taken as precise theoretical formulations. The biblical authors affirm that since God is the creator and lord of history, all events flow directly or indirectly from God's will, and that no events can decisively frustrate God's ultimate purpose. This conviction appears sometimes in the form of assertions that God acts directly in all events. These passages, however, cannot be interpreted to mean that God is the sole agent in the creation. The authors of Exodus, for example, variously assert that God hardened Pharaoh's heart (4:21, 7:3, 14:4), or that Pharaoh hardened his own heart (8:32, 9:34), or simply and indefinitely that Pharaoh's heart was hardened (9:35).

The events which are most clearly not providential in the sense defined are those involving sin or the human rebellion against God and disobedience to the divine will. In no sense can these events be characterized as participating in the divine will to bring all people to their fulfillment. In the Bible God is said to be angry or grieved or saddened by such events (Gen. 6:6). Over and over again it is recorded that "the anger of the Lord was kindled against Israel" because of its sin (see, for example, Num. 25:3, 32:13, Josh. 7:1, 2 Sam. 24:1, 2 Kings 13:3, Isa. 5:25). It may be as it is sometimes affirmed in the Bible that such actions fall within the divine foreknowledge and in this sense within the divine plan, and that God can redeem sin and bring good out of evil. However, to assert that sinful actions in themselves are providential in the sense defined is contradictory and makes no sense.

This is made even clearer in the New Testament in the idea of the evil spiritual powers. These are angelic creatures who have rebelled against God and fallen from grace into sin and now rule the world and cause evil events. The author of Ephesians states that we are contending "against the prinicipalities, against the powers, against the world rulers of this present darkness, against the spiritual hosts of wickedness in the heavenly places" (6:12, see also 2:2, Jn. 12:31, 16:11, 14:30, 1 Cor. 2:6, 8, 2 Cor. 4:4, Gal. 4:8). Although Christ has broken the power of these beings in principle, they still cause illness, persecution, and other calamities. Although the new age has dawned, in the present it overlaps with the old age in which the evil powers are still at work. The actions of these evil powers are by definition opposed to God's rule and to the divine will to bring all people to their fulfillment. This view was generally affirmed in the tradition down to the modern period when it was denied by the liberal theology and then reaffirmed by neo-orthodoxy and evangelicalism.

It is asserted in the Bible and the tradition that God can and does redeem and bring good out of evil events. However, does this mean that the evil events themselves are providential in the sense defined? Only if it is argued that the evil events are somehow willed by God as part of the divine plan for the world. There is no evidence for such a view in the Bible, although it was occasionally argued in the tradition.

I conclude that the evidence for the second answer is stronger than that for the first, and that therefore not all events are providential.

Comment: This question indicates that some issues can be resolved by analysis alone without argument. This usually results from the analysis of a key term. An example of this can be found in the treatment by John Wilson of the question, Ought punishment to be retributive?[6] He concludes from his analysis of ordinary usage that unless punishment is retributive, it is not considered punishment. The quality of being retributive is involved in the very meaning of the concept of punishment. Thus the question is resolved by analysis, and it is not necessary to investigate arguments for and against punishment being made retributive. In our question this was the case in the analysis of "equally." However, in order to pursue the question to the stage of argument, we chose to drop "equally" from the question.

8

Humanity

What is the relation of body and soul?

This question has concerned Christians from the beginning. The original tension between Hellenistic doubts about the body and the positive implications of the Christian belief in creation, incarnation, and the resurrection of the body raised issues for Christian faith which have exercised Christian thinkers in every century. One aspect of this, the mind-body problem, has perplexed philosophers from Aristotle to the present. Some contemporary theologians argue that the body has been unduly depreciated in relation to the soul in Christian history and that it must be seen as equal if not superior to the soul. So the question seems to be of perennial interest, and especially at the present time.

The meaning of the question hangs on the interpretation of the terms "soul" and "body." The soul can refer to the principle of vitality of the body, that which humans share with other animals or "souled" beings. It can also refer to the uniquely human capacities of self-transcendence, reason, and will, or it can refer to both of these together. When it is taken to refer only to the first of these, the term "spirit" is commonly used to refer to the second.

This raises the issue of whether or not this is a theological question. Is it a question about God or the world in relation to God? It does not seem to be. However, if the concept of soul involves a relation to God, then it is a theological question. The question is not whether the soul is related to God, since everything is related to God. Rather the question is, Does the *concept* of soul involve a relation to God?

Let us look at its two aspects. The question about the relation of the body to its principle of vitality would seem to be a biological question about the internal structure of the human being. To be sure it was discussed by theologians down into the nineteenth century. In the eighteenth century, however, the empirical science of psychology began to be distinguished from philosophy and theology. And one of the issues which it considered was that of the relation of the body to the structure and processes of the animal soul, as it was called. So this is not a theological question.

The other aspect of the concept of the soul, the uniquely human capacities of self-transcendence, reason, and will, has always been understood in the theological tradition to involve a relation to God. For example, in most of the tradition the soul was understood to be the image of God and to be created directly by God rather than through the parents. Therefore, I conclude that the question of the relation of this aspect of the soul, namely, the spirit, to the body is a theological issue. So let us interpret the question to be, What is the relation of body and spirit?

Another complication in the question derives from unclarity about the concept of the body. The body may be interpreted as the living body, in which case it includes the first aspect of the concept of the soul. Or the body may be interpreted as the physico-chemical body as distinct from its vitality. (The definition of the body as the living body is modern and appears first in Descartes. Previous thinkers generally understood the body as the physico-chemical body.) Since in a living person the question of the relation body in this latter sense and the spirit is rather abstract and of no special interest, the concept of the body is best understood to include the first aspect of the soul. So let us interpret the question further to be, What is the relation between the living body and the spirit?

A final complication arises when we inquire about the context in which the question is raised. It may be that the relation of body and spirit is different in the states or orders of creation, sin, salvation, and fulfillment.[1] Let us assume that the question is asking about the present relation of living body and spirit in Christians. Since this is a complex situation involving the states of creation, sin, and salvation, the relation in each of these states will have to be explored.

The state of creation refers to that intended by God the creator apart from sin. The state of sin refers to the state of estrangement "after" the fall or rebellion of humanity against God and "before" salvation. This is a state of alienation from the state of creation and involves estrangement from God, the world, neighbors, and from one's true humanity. The state of salvation refers to the historical state of restoration of communion with God, the world, neighbors, and one's true humanity. It is realized only fragmentarily in history. The state of fulfillment refers to the final or eschatological state in the reign of God in which salvation is complete.

The states of creation and fulfillment can be spoken of only mythologically, since they transcend the historical situation of humanity. In some theologies they are identified; in others they are not. The state of sin is in itself abstract in the sense that existential estrangement in the disruption of a given created state which is essentially good. It is also considered abstract in some theologies which assert that it is always partially overcome by the presence in varying degrees of the state of salvation. Although other theologies deny this, they would affirm it in the case of Christians, which is the situation addressed in our question. Thus the situation of Christians is one combining essential created goodness, existential estrangement from this, fragmentary participation in salvation, which is the overcoming of the latter, and hope for the fulfillment of salvation which is proleptically present.

Now we can rephrase the question as follows: What is the relation between the living body and the spirit in Christians? What are the possible answers to this question? The various philosophical discussions of the mind-body problem are not much help here. They are generally using definitions of mind and body which are different from our definitions of spirit and living body. They do not consider the various theological states mentioned above since they are concerned only with the formal relation. All the monistic theories which deny that there are two realities to be related are ruled out by the doctrines of creation and humanity which affirm the reality of both spirit and living body in the sense that neither can be reduced to the other. None of the dualistic theories (occasionalism, parallelism, epiphenomenalism, and interactionism) seems to be coherent with the Christian view of human freedom except the last which affirms that the body can affect the mind and vice versa. This, however, is a formal answer to the question and leaves open several possibilities.

The possible answers are as follows:

1. The relation of the living body and the spirit in Christians is one of tension and conflict.

2. The relation of the living body and the spirit in Christians is one of equal partnership, interdependence, and complementarity.

3. The relation of the living body and the spirit in Christians is one of hierarchy in which the spirit is the predominant center of the person and, although dependent upon the body, acts and expresses itself in and through the body.

Our procedure on this question will be to investigate each possible answer in turn.

1. The relation of the living body and the spirit in Christians is one of tension and conflict. According to the Bible humanity is constituted by two distinct principles, dust and soul or spirit. "Then the Lord God formed man of dust from the ground, and breathed into his nostrils the breath of life" (Gen. 2:7). The body is seen as the lower part of human nature which weighs down the soul or spirit (Wisd. 9:15). According to the synoptic authors Jesus saw life as a struggle between these two principles. "The spirit indeed is willing, but the flesh is weak" (Mk. 14:38). Paul described this tension between the body or flesh and the spirit in great detail. "The desires of the flesh are against the spirit, and the desires of the spirit are against the flesh; for these are opposed to each other" (Gal. 5:17). "I delight in the law of God in my inmost self, but I see in my

members another law at war with the law of my mind and making me captive to the law of sin which dwells in my members'' (Rom. 7:22-23; see Rom. 8:13, 1 Cor. 15:50, 2 Cor. 5:1, Jn. 6:63).

This theme is continued in the early church authors who generally taught that humanity is constituted by an immortal soul and a mortal body. After some debate the official view became that of creationism: the body is produced by the parents, but the soul is created directly by God at the moment of conception. The main problem of the Christian life is the struggle of the soul or spirit against the sinful passions which have their seat in the body. It is the struggle of the soul or spirit to free itself from the body. The second century Letter to Diognetus asserts that the flesh hates the soul which is shut up in the body as a prison.[2] A human being, says Clement of Alexandria is like

> the Centaur, a Thessalian figment, compounded of a rational and an irrational part, of soul and body. Well, the body tills the ground, and hastes to it; but the soul is raised to God: trained in the true philosophy, it speeds to its kindred above, turning away from the lusts of the body. . . . The severance, therefore, of the soul from the body, made a life-long study, produces in the philosopher gnostic [Christian] alacrity, so that he is easily able to bear natural death, which is the dissolution of the chains which bind the soul to the body.[3]

Origen even spoke of the body as a punishment for the soul.[4] A fourth century desert ascetic is reported to have said that if the body is strong, the soul withers, and if the body withers, the soul is strong. Augustine occasionally taught that the body is like a cage and is our heaviest bond. It is universally taught that the image of God is found not in the body but in the soul or spirit, the higher and nobler part of human nature.

Thus in the Christian life the relation of the living body and the spirit is one of tension and conflict which is fragmentarily overcome when the spirit tames and controls the passions of the body in preparation for their separation at death.

2. The relation of the living body and the spirit in Christians is one of equal partnership, interdependence, and complementarity. The Old Testament view of the human being is a holistic and integrated one. The living body and the spirit are not set over against each other but rather refer to the whole person from different points of view. The usages of the terms for soul (*nephesh*), spirit (*ruach*), and heart (*leb*), as well as other parts of the body all overlap and are often interchangeable.

Soul means simply life, is attributed to animals as well as humans, and is especially associated with breath and blood (Gen. 1:30, 2:7, 9:4, Lev. 17:11, 14, 24:18, Deut. 12:23). The soul can refer to individuals themselves (Gen. 14:21, Ps. 42:5, 62:5, 103:1, Jer. 43:6), and to the seat of all wishes, desires, feelings, and emotions, even longing for and exulting in God (Ps. 25:1, 35:9, 86:4, 143:8, 146:1, Isa. 61:10). Soul and spirit refer to the whole person seen from somewhat different points of view (Isa. 26:9).

The parts of the body have psychological and spiritual functions. The heart is the seat of the emotions, the subject of intellectual and volitional processes, and the point of contact with God (Job 12:3, Ps. 27:8, Prov. 6:18, 27:11). It can refer simply to persons themselves (Ps. 27:3). The kidneys, bowels, liver, bones, and flesh function similarly. Only the head is missing!

Thus in the Old Testament the human person is an animated body and not an incarcerated soul (H. W. Robinson). Persons do not *have* bodies; they *are* bodies (J. A. T. Robinson). The body is simply the soul in its outward form (Pedersen). Hebrew thought was not concerned with the relations of parts of the person, but with the relation of the whole person, body, soul, and spirit, to God.

Likewise in the New Testament spirit (*pneuma*), soul (*psyche*), body (*soma*), and flesh (*sarx*) each refer to the whole person under different aspects. Jesus' teaching about the relation of the living body and the spirit as presented in the synoptic gospels is very close to that of the Old Testament. Body or flesh can refer to the whole person (Mt. 5:29, 6:22, Mk. 13:20), as can soul or spirit (Mk. 8:12, 35, 10:45, 14:34, Lk. 1:80, 8:55).

Paul's usage is more complex. Body and flesh refer to the whole person from the point of view of physical existence (1 Cor. 13:3, 2 Cor. 7:5, 10:10, Col 1:24; see Eph. 5:28-29) from the point of view of weakness and mortality (Rom. 6:19, Gal. 4:13), and from the point of view of involvement in sin (Rom. 6:6, 7:5, 24, 8:5, 7, 13). The flesh is not essentially physical or sensual, since the works of the flesh are primarily spiritual in character (Gal. 5:19-21). The body is very close to our word "personality" (Rom. 12:1, 1 Cor. 6:19-20, Phil. 1:28; see Eph. 5:28-29), and can refer simply to the self (Rom. 6:12-13, 1 Cor. 6:15). The main difference is that the body in distinction from the flesh has the possibility of a positive relation to God through Christ (1 Cor. 6:13-20).

The soul can mean simply life (Phil. 2:30), or it can refer to the self (2 Cor. 1:23, 1 Thess. 2:8). It can mean natural or physical in contrast to spiritual (1 Cor. 2:14, 15:44-45). The spirit is the whole person as open to God (Rom. 8:16, 1 Cor. 2:11). References is one passage to body, soul, and spirit (1 Thess. 5:23; see 1 Cor. 7:34) do not mean that Paul holds that a human being is a composite of three elements. They rather serve to emphasize that it is the whole person which is being referred to.

The theological tradition of the church tended to fall away from the biblical view of the equal partnership of living body and spirit, but there is a strand of the tradition which remained faithful to the biblical view.

Tertullian, for example, held that the flesh is the "pivot" of salvation, the soul's link with God, that which makes possible the soul's election by God, the consort and co-heir with the soul in things temporal and eternal.[5] Augustine described the body as the spouse of the soul.[6] Gregory of Nyssa affirmed that both body and soul participate in the image of God. Thomas Aquinas denied that the soul is the person and that the soul uses the body; the soul is simply the form of the body.[7]

In contemporary theology the unity of the person is being recovered. There is a renewed emphasis on the centrality of feeling as the response of the whole person, body and spirit, to reality and thus on the equal partnership of living body and spirit in the unity of the person.[8]

3. The relation of the living body and the spirit in Christians is one of hierarchy in which the spirit is the predominant center of the person and, although dependent upon the body, acts and expresses itself in and through the body. The first two answers are exaggerations and misinterpretations of themes in the Bible and the tradition. In general the first answer interprets the obvious duality of living body and spirit as a moral and metaphysical dualism and conflict.

Whatever tension and conflict there is, however, is that within the divided spirit. It is the result of the misdirection of the desires by the spirit, and not a conflict between the spirit and the desires which have their seat in the living body. Whatever tension and conflict is attested is the result of sin which involves alienation from one's true humanity and disruption of the person. It is not the result of a moral or metaphysical dualism of body and spirit. Furthermore, sin has its seat in the spirit and not in the body. It is the turning away of the person from God in disobedience. Thus the occasional dualism and tension found in the tradition derives from the influence of Hellenistic philosophy, from a misinterpretation of the analysis of the situation of sin, and from distinctions made in the attempt to integrate body and spirit in the light of the doctrines of creation, incarnation, and resurrection of the body.[9]

The second answer, on the other hand, constitutes an exaggeration of the biblical emphasis on the integrity of the human person. The fluidity of the biblical ideas of body, flesh, soul, and spirit is derived from the variety of authors involved, the millenium span of the writings, the lack of systematic concern, and the overriding insight into the unity of the human being. When the biblical view is considered as a whole, however, a clearly hierarchical picture emerges.

It is argued in the second answer that the various terms for living body and spirit refer to the whole person from different points of view or under different aspects. These different points of view and different aspects, however, constitute a hierarchy in which the living body is subordinate to the spirit which is the predominant center of the person. In the Old Testament the spirit, whether it is referred to by *nephesh* or *ruach*, is understood to be the central organ of the psychic life and thus as the mind, the will, and the means of the relation to God (Isa. 26:9, Jer. 51:11, Hag. 1:14).

The situation is the same in the New Testament. This is obscured by the fact that *soma* and *sarx* do not refer to the living body but rather to the whole person seen from certain points of view. If "flesh" means the whole person turned away from God, then it does not refer to the living body but rather to the spirit as the dominant center of the person. If "body" is close to our modern concept of personality or self, then it also does not refer to the living body, but rather to the spirit.

The overwhelming testimony of the tradition is to a hierarchical view of the relation of living body and spirit. This is partially the result of the influence of Hellenistic philosophy, but it is also an accurate interpretation of the biblical writings. Augustine's formulation is typical: "Just as the soul is the whole life of the body, so God is the blessed life of the soul."[10] Aquinas argues that since the proper operation of a human being is to understand, the intellectual principle or soul is the form of a human being and thus the form of the body.[11] According to Calvin the soul is the nobler part, the primary seat of the divine image, and the source of all activity in the person.[12]

The most careful treatment of this issue in this century is that of Paul Tillich. Although he rejects a hierarchical picture of life with its grades or levels of being, the view he develops is hierarchical in the sense discussed above. In the multidimensional unity of life there is an order of the dimensions: inorganic, organic (vegetative, animal), psychological, and spiritual. Those dimensions which precede are the necessary conditions of those which follow, and the latest dimension to emerge is always dominant in the individual. Thus the emergence of the dimension of spirit is dependent upon the presence of the inorganic, organic, and psychological dimensions, and where the dimension of spirit appears it is dominant over the others.[13]

The danger of hierarchy in the relation of spirit to living body is that when the spirit is distorted by sin, it can exercise its predominance in such a way that the harmony of the dimensions is disrupted. The romantic solution to this problem, as seen in the second answer, is to reduce the spirit to the living body. This, however, is impossible, since it is a free act which thus denies the solution and which can result only in the disruption of the person.

Therefore, I conclude that the third answer is the correct one, and that the relation of the living body and the spirit is Christians is a hierarchical one in which the spirit is the predominant center of the person which acts and expresses itself in and through the living body as its medium or instrument.

⑨

Sin

What is the relation of sin and neurosis?

The concept of neurosis is one of the main modern ways of speaking of the problematic character of the human situation, the source of human unhappiness and evil. The traditional Christian way of speaking of this is the concept of sin. So the question naturally arises about the relation of these two concepts. The question might occur to someone who wonders whether neurosis is simply a modern scientific way of talking about a phenomenon which a pre-scientific mythological age called sin. The question is significant because it is one specific and important instance of the general question about the relation of theological and scientific concepts. Contemporary theology has been deeply influenced by psychological, and especially psychiatric, concepts. So the question of the relation of the two kinds of concepts is of fundamental importance for theology. More practically, a person who feels depressed, conflicted, and guilty may wonder whether this is caused by sin or neurosis and whether to go to a priest or a psychiatrist.

Now in this question are we inquiring about the relation of the concepts of neurosis and sin or about the relation of the two referents of the concepts, the phenomena to which the concepts refer? Let us interpret the question to be inquiring about the relation of the phenomena. However, we can understand this relation only by means of the concepts. So we are inquiring about the relation of the phenomena by means of our inquiry about the relation of the concepts. Let us assume some provisional working definitions of the concepts. Let us define neurosis as an unconscious emotional conflict arising from repression which inhibits the functioning of the personality. Let us define sin as estrangement from God resulting in estrangement from the self, the neighbor, and the world. These definitions raise other questions, but we can deal with these as they arise in the course of our inquiry.

Now what are the possible answers to this question? The possible answers are the logically possible relations between concepts. What are the possible relations between concepts? For our purposes in this question the logically possible relations between concepts are independence, inclusion or class membership, contradiction or mutual exclusion, identity, causality, and complementarity. Concepts may be independent or have no significant relation, as in the case of the concepts of gravity and democracy. Concepts may have the relation of inclusion or genus to species as in the case of the concepts of feeling and anger. Concepts may have a relation or contradiction, as in the case of the big-bang and steady-state theories of the universe. Concepts may be identical or equivalent, as in the case of the concepts of incarnation and embodiment, although this example may be debatable. Concepts may have the relation of causality, as in the case of the concepts of force and acceleration. And finally, concepts may have the relation of complementarity in the sense that they refer to two aspects of one reality, as in the case of the concepts of wave and particle in the theory of light.[1] Our procedure will be to explore each of these possible answers in turn.

Are the concepts of neurosis and sin independent of each other with no significant relation? We will note below a definite similarity and parallelism between them. So we will be able to conclude that they are independent only when we have explored and excluded all the other possibilities. Is the relation one of inclusion or genus to species? Is sin one type of neurosis, or is neurosis a kind of sin? No theologian has ever suggested this relation. Freud implied that the sense of estrangement from God is a kind of neurosis, but his theory is not very clear or consistent and was not pursued by his followers. This will be explored further below in connection with the relation of causality. So inclusion or class membership does not seem to be the proper relation between the concepts.

Are the concepts of sin and neurosis contradictory in the sense that if one is valid, the other must be invalid? This would be the case only if they referred to the same phenomena and were mutually exclusive interpretations of that phenomenon. Is sin perhaps a pre-scientific or mythological way of talking about something which psychiatry speaks of with the term neurosis? Pre-scientific concepts, such as that of a local heaven surrounding the earth, have been superseded by modern astronomical concepts, and theologians who accept modern astronomy no longer use the concept of a local heaven. However, theologians such as Roberts and Tillich who accept the validity of psychiatry still use the concept of sin. The concept of neurosis has not superseded the concept of sin except for those who would not accept any theological concepts. The concepts of sin and neurosis can be applied at the same time to one and the same person without contradiction. That is, it is possible for a person to have an unconscious emotional conflict and to be estranged from God at the same time. They may be present together in one person, or they may be different aspects of one state of a person, which would be the relation of complementarity. Therefore, the concepts of sin and neurosis are not contradictory in the sense of alternate or mutually exclusive interpretations of one state or phenomenon in a person.

Are the concepts of sin and neurosis identical? There are clearly a number of similarities between the concepts. David E. Roberts writes,

> At certain points there is a remarkable parallel between the Pauline-Augustinian conception of original sin and the psychoanalytical conception of neurosis. Freud more than once called attention to the parallel. In both instances man finds himself in a condition of inner conflict, and filled with hatred, envy and mistrust toward his neighbors. In both instances it is the basic condition that is enslaving; particular "sins" or "symptoms" are peripheral effects deriving from this central cause, and particular "good deeds" make little dent upon the basic condition. In both instances the injurious influences of others are seen to be so interwoven with personal reactions that it is almost impossible to differentiate between them. Similarly, it is almost impossible to disentangle the respects in which a man has fallen into sin (or neurosis) by necessity or through his own "fault." In both instances the central problem cannot be solved merely by an effort of the will; insofar as it ever gets solved at all, the solution comes about through a change in the "will" itself.[2]

Furthermore, both concepts refer to states of a person, the state of unconscious emotional conflict and the state of estrangement from God. However, these states are defined in terms of quite distinct sets of concepts and can be interpreted as distinct. That is, we can conceive of a state of estrangement from God which is not per se a state of unconscious emotional conflict, and vice versa. Therefore, the concepts do not seem to be identical.

Is the relation of the concepts of sin and neurosis one of causality? Is sin the cause of neurosis or neurosis the cause of sin? This can refer to sin and neurosis in one person or in different persons. That is, it can refer to sin in one person causing neurosis in the same person, or it can refer to sin in one person causing neurosis in another person, for example, a parent and a child. Let us interpret causality to refer to the relationship in one person.

A problem with the relation of causality is that it is part of the concepts of sin and neurosis that they are uncaused in some sense. For example, it is argued in the text that we cannot specify a cause of sin without explaining it away. Since sin is a matter of the will, it cannot be caused by something else without ceasing to be sin.[3] Something similar is usually asserted about neurosis, namely that it cannot be externally caused and still be neurosis, that a neurosis is always caused by repression which is in some sense an act of the person and not anyone else. However, since both sin and neurosis are self-caused in the sense of being acts of the will, they may be considered to be causally related in the same person. That is, the idea of neurosis causing sin does not contradict the element in the concept of sin which asserts that sin cannot be caused by anything else without explaining it away by relieving the sinner of responsibility. The same applies to the idea of sin causing neurosis.

In this sense it is conceivable that estrangement from God might cause unconscious emotional conflict directly or indirectly. Similarly it is conceivable that unconscious emotional conflict could be the cause of estrangement from God, because it is conceivable in the analogous situation of the relation between two people. That is, an unconscious emotional conflict in one person could be the cause of estrangement between this person and another person. Is this causal relation always the case? Probably not, because it is always possible to conceive the presence of sin without neurosis and vice versa.

Although the concept of neurosis was unknown before the late nineteenth century, there is an element in the Christian tradition which tends to support the causal relation between sin and neurosis. Paul taught that when a person rebels against God, this leads to the disruption of the person (Rom. 1:28-32). Similarly Augustine taught that when the will is not subordinate to God, the affections of the soul are insubordinate to the will and become disordered.[4] According to Christian faith a person's relation to God is fundamental to the person's well being on all levels, including the psychological. If the relation to God is disrupted, then we can expect things to begin to go wrong on all levels of the person's life. If persons are created to have their lives centered in God, then to lose this center is to place all aspects of life in jeopardy, leading to psychological confusion, conflict, and perhaps neurosis. Thus we have discovered that causality is a possible relation between the concepts of sin and neurosis.

Are these concepts complementary in the sense that they refer to different aspects of one reality in a person? Is it possible to assert that one particular human state looked at from one point of view is an unconscious emotional conflict and looked at from another point of view is estrangement from God? This sounds like a possibility. Ernest Becker writes,

> Here Rank and Kierkegaard meet in one of those astonishing historical mergers of thought: that sin and neurosis are two ways of talking about the same thing—the complete isolation of the individual, his disharmony with the rest of nature, his hyperindividualism, his attempt to create his own world from within himself. Both sin and neurosis represent the individual blowing himself up to larger than his true size, his refusal to recognize his cosmic dependence.[5]

And he quotes Otto Rank,

> The neurotic type suffers from a consciousness of sin just as much as did his religious ancestor, without believing in the concept of sin.

This is precisely what makes him "neurotic;" he feels a sinner without the religious belief in sin for which he therefore needs a new rational explanation.[6]

However, if, as we have noted above, it is possible to conceive of the presence of sin without neurosis and vice versa, then this complementary relation would not always be the case. So the concepts may be complementary but not necessarily always.

At this point it is important to note that the referents of the concepts of sin and neurosis are usually held to be universal, that is, present in all people. The Christian doctrine of sin asserts that estrangement from God is universal, and that it is overcome only fragmentarily in historical life.[7] Freud and his followers assert that neurosis in some form and in some degree is probably universal, but that it can be overcome in varying degrees. We have noted that one limitation of the applicability of the relations of causality and complementarity is the fact that it is possible to conceive the presence of sin without neurosis and vice versa. If, however, the concepts of sin and neurosis both involve their universality, then this limitation is removed.

Therefore, I conclude that the relation of sin and neurosis is most likely that of causality and complementarity. Now are these two relations themselves mutually exclusive or complementary? That is, can the relation of sin and neurosis be both causal and complementary, or must it be one or the other? It would seem that they can be understood as complementary, since it is possible to claim, for example, that sin causes neurosis and that this neurosis then becomes a complementary aspect of sin.

This is confirmed when we consider the ideal situation in regard to sin and neurosis. The absence of sin would mean the ideal relation to God, that is, faith or perfect trust and love. The absence of neurosis would mean no repression and thus no unconscious conflict. This would be occasioned by perfect trust and love in relation to others, especially for the infant and the parents. This in turn might be called the infantile form of faith. Thus, it is possible to argue that faith, which is the opposite of sin,[8] is the basis of the avoidance or overcoming of repression and thus neurosis.[9]

10

Christk

When Jesus prayed, who was praying to whom?

This question might arise for someone who sees the New Testament picture of Jesus as a man of prayer, who is aware of the christological tradition which asserts that Jesus is fully divine, and who wonders whether and how they hang together. The coherence of this tradition with the New Testament picture of Jesus is probably widely doubted today. Thus this question raises in a sharp way the relation of Jesus to God, especially in the most intimate area of this relationship. It also poses the question of whether Jesus was really one of us, truly shared our human situation before God, or whether he is a divine being with whom we cannot really identify.

I interpret the question to be asking who is the subject and who is the object of Jesus' prayer, who is really praying and who is hearing this prayer. There can be little doubt that Jesus often prayed to God. The gospels attest that Jesus prayed and taught his disciples to pray (Mk. 1:35, 6:46, 15:34, Lk. 3:21, 5:16, 6:12, 9:18, 29, 10:21, 11:1, 22:41-44, 23:34, 46 par. Jn. 11:41, 12:27, 17:1-26).

The possible answers to this question are as follows:

1. A man praying to the triune God.
2. Christ's human nature praying to his divine nature.
3. God the Son praying to God the Father.
4. A man fully inspired by the Holy Spirit praying to the triune God.

Our procedure will be to investigate each possible answer in turn.

1. A man praying to the triune God. On the face of it the New Testament picture of Jesus at prayer is simply that of a man praying to God (Lk. 6:12). Is it appropriate to describe God here as the triune God? The New Testament attests a God who is in some sense triune (Mt. 28:19, 2 Cor. 13:14, Gal. 4:6, 1 Pet. 1:2), and the fourth century doctrine of the trinity is one interpretation of this. Since we shall have to choose some interpretation of this testimony in order to answer the question, let us assume the traditional one as interpreted in the western tradition.[1]

It may be objected that this answer is anachronistic, that Jesus of course knew nothing of the doctrine of the trinity. However, I interpret the question to refer not to Jesus' understanding of his prayer but rather ours. If we affirm that God is triune in some sense, we must affirm that God was triune in the first century as well as the fourth and the twentieth. Furthermore, it can be argued that since Jesus often spoke of God as Father and of the Word and Spirit of God, he was aware of what may be called the raw materials of the doctrine of the trinity, and that what was implicit in his understanding and in that of the early Christians was made explicit later.

However, the New Testament testimony is more complicated than the simple picture of the man Jesus praying to the triune God, because it also affirms that Jesus is the Lord, the Son of God, the image of God, in the form of God, the one in whom the fullness of God dwells, and the one through whom and for whom all things were created (1 Cor. 12:3, Mt. 16:16, 2 Cor. 4:4, Phil. 2:6, Col. 1:15, 19). Thus Jesus' relation to God is not simply that of a man before the triune God. Therefore, the first answer is inadequate as it stands.

2. Christ's human nature praying to his divine nature. The meaning of this answer depends upon how we interpret the two natures of Christ and their relation. A relationship involving communication, such as prayer, requires two distinct terms. Therefore, the less the unity of the two natures is emphasized, as in Nestorianism, the more intelligible is the relation of prayer in this answer. The Nestorian view of the relation of the two natures of Christ is that there is a moral union between them, but this view was condemned by the church at the council of Ephesus in 431. The more the unity of the two natures is emphasized, as in the formula of the council of Chalcedon, the less intelligible is the relation involved in Jesus' prayer.

The traditional view of the relation of the two natures of Christ as stated in the Chalcedonian formula is that of the hypostatic union which is without confusion, change, division, or separation. The relation of prayer necessarily involves some distinction between subject and object but not necessarily any division or separation. So the traditional view allows the possibility of this answer, but since it is quite formal in character it is not very illuminating for the meaning of this answer.

In any case the affirmation of the unity of the person of Christ in the traditional view makes this answer difficult to understand. Moreover, one element in the traditional view was that, since Jesus Christ was one person and this one person was that of God the Son, therefore Jesus' human nature was impersonal or *anhypostatos*. This would make this answer to our question unintelligible. Finally, the overwhelming testimony of the New Testament is that Jesus' prayer was addressed to the Father rather than to the Son of God. Therefore this second answer is also inadequate.

3. God the Son incarnate praying to God the Father. Throughout the New Testament Jesus is identified as the Son of God. So it would seem to

follow that Jesus' prayer is that of the Son to the Father. The doctrine of the trinity elaborated by the early eastern Christian authors and also by the modern social analogy school, as represented by Hodgson and Moltmann, is able to interpret this answer successfully. Since the "persons" of the trinity are analogically persons in the modern sense, then the relation of Jesus to God is in fact the relation of God the Son to God the Father.

The main problem with this answer is that it implies that the "persons" of the trinity are parts of God on the analogy of a family. The theological tradition, however, has generally denied that the "persons" are parts of God and affirmed rather than they are modes of the whole godhead, as in the analogy of one who is parent, spouse, and citizen.[2] This interpretation of the doctrine of the trinity is less able to make sense of this answer to our question. Can one mode of God speak to another? In the analogy can one's whole being as parent speak to one's whole being as citizen? This is conceivable in terms of human self-transcendence and self-reflection, but it does not seem to do justice to the relation of prayer. It must be remembered, however, that Jesus's experience of prayer was undoubtedly not one of communicating with a little known and distant deity as other human prayer often is. It was probably the most intimate kind of communion in which God's presence was so immediate that the most intimate kinds of human communion are only remote analogies of it.

Another difficulty with the third answer, however, is that it implies that Jesus is identical with God the Son. This was a hotly debated issue in the tradition, but the view that Jesus' mind or spirit was that of God the Son was condemned as Appollinarianism at the council of Constantinople in 381. Appollinaris was alleged to have taught that Jesus had no human mind or spirit, because this had been replaced by God the Son. In condemning this view the church affirmed that Jesus was fully human and had a complete human nature. For these reasons the third answer does not seem adequate.

4. A man fully inspired by the Holy Spirit praying to the triune God. In the New Testament Jesus is depicted as being conceived, moved, guided, and empowered by the Holy Spirit (Mt. 1:18, 12:28, Mk. 1:9-12, Lk. 1:35, 4:1, 14, 18, 21). Thus one of the earliest layers of tradition in the interpretation of Christ has been called a Spirit christology.[3] Jesus is the one who is fully and perfectly indwelt by the Holy Spirit. Since the Spirit also indwells Christians, their experience of the presence and working of the Spirit, when taken to the absolute degree, can be interpreted to be the relation of Jesus to God.[4] According to Paul the Holy Spirit inspires Christian prayer and even prays in Christian prayer (Rom. 8:26-27). Thus Christian prayer has traditionally been understood to be addressed to God the Father, through God the Son, and in God the Holy Spirit. So Jesus' prayer to God would be in principle no more difficult to understand than our own prayer.

This is mysterious, but it may not be as far from our experience as we may think. We have all had the experience of being moved by the presence and love of a good friend to speak to this friend about some issue of great import to us. There is no contradiction in this. The friend is not simply speaking to himself or herself but rather inspires us to speak.

However, if Jesus is moved by the full and perfect indwelling of the Holy Spirit to address the triune God, does not this involve considering the "persons" of the trinity as parts of God? The analogy of the good friend indicates that being inspired by the Spirit to address the triune God does not involve this difficulty as much as the idea of God the Son addressing God the Father. And in theology, other things being equal, we have to settle for the lesser difficulty.

Therefore, I conclude that on the whole the fourth answer is the most satisfactory.

11

Salvation

What is the relation between Christian salvation and liberation from social, economic, and political oppression?

This question is one of the main points of debate between liberation theologians and other theologians. Many liberation theologians maintain that salvation is identical with liberation from social, economic, and political oppression. They claim that the understanding of salvation has been spiritualized by the oppressors and those who have a stake in the status quo. Other theologians argue the salvation is fundamentally spiritual and is centered on reconciliation with God.

I interpret the question to be inquiring about the relation between the concepts of salvation and liberation, and not between the concepts of salvation held by liberation and other theologians. The former requires the clarification of the two concepts, while the latter would require a survey of the writings of various theologians in order to compare their doctrines of salvation.

First, therefore, we need some working definitions of oppression, liberation, and salvation. In determining these definitions, however, we must be careful to follow general contemporary usage and to avoid resolving the question simply by these definitions. This latter would be done by using formulations which follow the line of argument of one point of view on the issue. For example, salvation could be defined as liberation from oppression thus by definition resolving the question with the answer of identity. Or the concepts could be defined in mutually exclusive terms which would resolve the question by definition with the answer of independence or contradiction. Some questions are questions of definition, such as, What is the meaning of salvation? Our question could be interpreted in that way, but it need not be.[1]

Let us define oppression as unjust limitation, restraint or discrimination in regard to the exercise of social relations, civil rights, and political liberties, for example in relation to marriage, housing, employment, political action, and recreation. Let us define liberation as the removal of all such unjust limitation, restraint and discrimination. Let us define salvation as well-being in the most comprehensive sense: physical, psychological, social, and spiritual. This is vague, but it has considerable basis in the Bible and the tradition.

One other aspect of the question needs clarification. Does the question refer to the situation in history or in the final fulfillment? In history all salvation and liberation are presumably fragmentary and may be lost, but in the final fulfillment they will both presumably be complete. Since the focus of concern in this question is probably on the historical situation, let us interpret it in that way.

Now what are the possible answers to this question? The possible answers are the logically possible relations between concepts.[2]

1. Independence. Salvation and liberation have no significant relation at all.

2. Contradiction. Where salvation is affirmed or present, liberation must be denied or is absent, and vice versa.

3. Identity. Salvation and liberation are identical.

4. Causality. Salvation causes liberation or vice versa.

5. Complementarity. Salvation and liberation are two aspects or parts of the same reality.

6. Inclusion. Salvation is part of liberation or vice versa.

The method which would seem to be the most economical in pursuing this question is to explore the meaning of salvation in the Bible and the tradition and then to determine which of the possible answers is most coherent with this.

In the Old Testament the model or type of salvation is the deliverance from bondage in Egypt, and the guidance through the wilderness and into the promised land (Deut. 6:21-23, 7:8-9, 26:2-10). This pattern is seen again and again in the history of Israel as deliverance from national peril, from defeat at the hand of enemies, and from exile. It came to include deliverance from individual and social perils and the providing of peace, justice, prosperity, health, and long life. All this is the doing of God (Ps. 3, 79), and it is all based on God's righteousness, the divine outgoing mercy, the divine faithfulness to the covenant, and the divine love for Israel and the world (Deut. 7:7-9, Isa. 45:21-23). This requires Israel's repentance, faith, trust, amendment, and obedience to the will of God. Such obedience includes the faithful participation of the people in the sacrificial cultus which involves the recital of God's deliverance and restores the relation to God under the covenant (Ex. 12:21-27, Deut. 26:1-11). Thus salvation is founded on the faithfulness of God who will vindicate Israel and restore it to the status of the children of God in the covenant. Finally salvation will be fully realized only in a future divine reign of peace, justice, and prosperity either in a millenial kingdom on earth or in a transformed creation, a new heaven and a new earth beyond history (Isa. 65:17-25, 66:22-23).

In Jesus' teaching and ministry salvation means essentially participation in the reign of God, but the focus is on the forgiveness of sin, reconciliation with God, and restoration to wholeness through the healing of disease and the casting out of demons (Mk. 2:1-12, Lk. 7:48-50, 11:20-22). The reign of God is the new age which is breaking in Jesus' preaching and healing. Salvation is entering the reign of God through repentance and faith and participating in the power of the new age.

In the Pauline and Johannine literature salvation is understood to be participation in the action of God in the life, ministry, death, and resurrection of Christ and the gift of the Spirit (Jn. 1:14-18, 3:14-18, Rom. 5:1-11). This participation involves justification or the forgiveness of sin through the sacrifice of Christ, reconciliation and communion with God, and new or eternal life in the power of the Holy Spirit (Rom. 3:21-26, 2 Cor. 5:16-20, 1 Jn. 1:7-2:2, 4:9-14). But this salvation in history is only a foretaste of the fullness and completion of salvation which will be accomplished at the return of Christ in glory and the resurrection of the dead. This final salvation will be cosmic in scope such that all things will be reconciled to God in a new creation, a new heaven and earth (Rom. 8:18-23, 1 Cor. 15:20-28, Eph. 1:10, Phil. 3:20, Col. 1:20, Rev. 21:1-22:5). Throughout the New Testament as well as the Old Testament the images of the final fulfillment are social and political in character: the messianic banquet, the heavenly city of the new Jerusalem, and the reign of God in which there will be justice and peace (Mt. 8:11, Lk. 13:29, Rev. 21).

Thus between the Old Testament and the New Testament there is at least a difference of emphasis in the understanding of salvation. In the New Testament the national dimension of the Old Testament view of salvation has disappeared, and the emphasis on political and military deliverance and economic well-being has moved into the background, except in the eschaton where it is fulfilled. For example, while in the Old Testament deliverance from enemies and political oppression is expected and received in history, in the New Testament such deliverance is mentioned only in the Book of Revelation where it occurs in the eschaton (Rev. 17-18). Christians under persecution and imprisonment were considered to be participants in salvation. To be sure in the early Christian community there is sharing of resources to care for those in need (Acts 4:32-37, 1 Cor. 16:1-4), but there is no concern for unjust economic and political structures as there is in the Old Testament. Moreover the concern for the needy in the New Testament is understood not as part of God's action of salvation but rather as part of the responsibility of the Christian life which flows from salvation.

The example of slavery is revealing. In the Old Testament the people of Israel are delivered by God from slavery in Egypt, but later they themselves keep slaves. The law required that all slaves be freed every seven or fifty years depending on the type of slavery, but this was largely honored in the breach. In the New Testament the institution of slavery is accepted, and the presence of slaves in the church is taken for granted. Slaves are to be accepted as brothers and sisters (Philem. 16), because in Christ the slave and the free person are one (1 Cor. 12:13, Gal. 3:28, Col. 3:11). Thus slaves are counseled to render faithful service to their masters (1 Cor. 7:20-24, Eph. 6:5-9). In the New Testament, therefore, deliverance from slavery is not seen as part of Christian salvation, except perhaps in the final consummation.

Therefore, it has been argued that the New Testament has spiritualized salvation by reducing it to reconciliation with God or at least that the tradition of the church has interpreted it this way.[3] What is clear is that while in the Old Testament the deliverance from bondage in Egypt is central, in the New Testament it is entrance into the reign of God, reconciliation with God, and eternal life which have become central. Liberation from oppression and the establishment of justice have become part of the task and responsibility of the Christian life, and their fulfillment has been referred to the eschaton. The Old Testament has a broader view of salvation than the New Testament, or, to put it the other way around, the New Testament has a sharper focus in its understanding of salvation. The New Testament has referred some aspects of the Old Testament view of salvation to the task of the Christian life and for their fulfillment to the consummation of history. When we find a difference in emphasis between the Old Testament and the New Testament, we can use the Old Testament to elaborate the meaning of the New Testament, but we must read the Old Testament in the light of the New Testament, because it is the testimony to the fulfillment in Christ of the promises of the Old Testament (Mt. 5:17, Heb. 1:1-2).

Although we cannot survey the various interpretations of salvation in the history of the church, it is clear that this tradition has largely followed the emphases of the New Testament rather than the Old Testament. Salvation has usually been understood to consist of forgiveness of sin, reconciliation with God, and participation in the divine life. Liberation from oppression has been a subordinate theme in the tradition, but it has referred primarily to liberation from sin, death, the law, the devil, and demonic powers rather than from social, economic, and political oppression, except where the latter has been understood as a manifestation of the former. The latter has become an explicit theme in the doctrine of salvation only in the past century in the theology of the social gospel, the theology of hope, and political and liberation theologies.

Now let us consider which of the above answers is most coherent with view of salvation we have outlined.

1. Independence. Because these concepts are closely related in the Bible, especially in the Old Testament, they cannot be considered independent.

2. Contradiction. It is clear that there is sufficient overlapping between the concepts of salvation and liberation to rule out their being contradictory.

3. Identity. Although in some passages of the Old Testament salvation and liberation seem to be identical, it is the consensus of both Old Testament and New Testament that salvation involves more than liberation and that salvation is focussed on reconciliation with God whereas liberation is not. Therefore, the concepts are not identical.

4. Causality. There are no grounds for arguing that liberation from oppression causes salvation in the sense of reconciliation with God. It could be claimed, however, on the basis of some parts of the Bible that salvation caused liberation in the sense that it supplies the basis and motivation for it in the Christian life. So causality is a partial answer to the question.

5. Complementarity. On the basis of certain passages in the Old Testament it can be argued that salvation and liberation are complementary, two aspects of the same reality looked at from different points of view. That is, salvation is reconciliation with God, and liberation from oppression is the social aspect of this reconciliation. The consensus of the biblical authors, however, seems to be that salvation is more comprehensive than reconciliation with God, and that liberation from oppression does not necessarily accompany salvation and may occur apart from it. Therefore, complementarity does not appear to be the correct answer.

6. Inclusion. It seems to be the consensus of the biblical authors that salvation includes liberation, that liberation is part of salvation understood as well-being in the most comprehensive sense. The limitation of this answer is the point we noted in connection with the answer of causality. If salvation is in any sense the cause of liberation, then it does not include liberation as part of it. The consensus of the New Testament is that while salvation is total well-being, its focus and foundation is the spiritual dimension, reconciliation with God and participation in the divine life.

Of the other dimensions of salvation, some, in particular the physical, psychological, and the more interpersonal aspects of the social dimension, receive their foundation in the spiritual dimension of salvation, are increased in sanctification understood as the process of salvation, and also constitute part of the task of the Christian life in the sense of the responsibility to help those in need. The economic and political dimensions of salvation and the more institutional aspects of the social dimension, which constitute liberation from oppression, when they are considered at all in the Bible and the tradition, constitute other parts of the task of the Christian life and receive their motivation from the spiritual dimension of salvation. In this series of dimensions we see an increasing dependence upon human mediation and activity and also therefore the increasingly fragmentary character of what can be achieved in history.

So in conclusion we can say that the relation between the concepts of salvation and liberation is partially causality but more clearly inclusion. The fundamental dimension of salvation which is reconciliation with God and participation in the divine life can be called the cause of liberation in that it constitutes the foundation of the Christian life and thus of motivation for carrying out the task of liberation from oppression. However, salvation understood as comprehensive well-being stands in a relation of inclusion to liberation from oppression.

12

Justification

Does justification mean primarily being accounted righteous or being made righteous?

This question was at the center of the Reformation debate between the Protestants and the Catholics. The Protestants argued that justification meant being accounted as righteous, and the Catholics argued that it meant being actually made righteous. Each side was pressed into exaggerations in opposition to the other. Each felt that a fundamental issue in the meaning of the gospel was at stake. However, the question is not simply of historical interest. It raises an issue which is at the heart of Christian faith. What must I do to be saved? How can I be right with God? Must I be a good person in order to be saved? Do I need to be changed in order to be right with God?

Let us assume that the term "justification" refers to Paul's idea of the gift of God in Christ. Since the question is inquiring about the proper meaning of this term, it should not be further defined at this point in such a way which would answer the question by definition. The meaning of justification hangs on the meaning of the term "righteous" and on how this is attributed to the Christian. In particular the question focuses on whether God accepts sinners as they are or whether they must be changed by grace in order to be accepted by God.

The possible answers to the questions are as follows:

1. Justification means primarily being accounted righteous.

2. Justification means primarily being made righteous.

3. Justification means both being accounted righteous and made righteous.

The procedure on this question will be to interpret these answers briefly, then to explore the biblical understanding of righteousness and justification, and finally to determine which answer is most coherent with the biblical view.

1. Justification means being accounted righteous. This answer means that God through Christ has forgiven sinners, thus treats them as righteous, and accepts them into fellowship. This involves the idea of imputed

righteousness in which the believer shares in the righteousness of Christ and thus is acceptable to God. The central theme of this answer is that Christians are accepted by God as they are, as sinners, and do not have to be changed by grace in order to be acceptable to God.

2. Justification means being made righteous. This answers means that God through Christ has forgiven sinners and given them the gift of grace by which they have faith, hope and love and thus are made actually righteous in the sense of fulfilling God's will for them. This means that in the process of being forgiven and accepted by God the Christian is changed by grace.

3. Justification means both being accounted righteous and being made righteous. This answer combines the first two and implies that being accounted righteous and being made righteous are complementary aspects of justification, that being accepted by God involves being changed by grace.

In the Old Testament "righteousness" generally means the fulfillment of the conditions of the covenant relationship between God and humanity. God is righteous because God is faithful to the covenant and wills to save the people of God (Isa. 45:21). People are righteous if they are faithful to the covenant which God has made with them, if they trust in God for their salvation (Gen. 15:6, Hab. 2:4, Ps. 37:39-40). It does not depend on their being without sin and obedient to the law (Ps. 40:11-12, 65:3, 103:11-12, 143:1-2). God will save the people of God even if they continue to be stubborn and do not turn to God (Isa. 46:12-13).

This understanding of righteousness is continued in the New Testament and is focussed on the new convenant which God has established in Jesus Christ. People are righteous if they accept God's saving action in Christ, the restored covenant relationship with God. Because the covenant has been broken by humanity, it cannot be restored by humanity even by keeping the law, that is by fulfilling the demands of the covenant. Therefore no one is righteous (Rom. 3:9-10, 20). However God in Christ has restored the covenant and made it possible for people to return to fellowship with God. This is accomplished by God in the righteousness of Christ manifest in his perfect obedience to God. This restores the covenant by fulfilling its demands (Rom. 3:21-26, 5:18-19). Human righteousness comes from accepting the new covenant with God through repentance and faith (Lk. 18:9-14). Thus Paul can state that Christ is our righteousness (1 Cor. 1:30) which comes to us as a gift (Rom. 3:24, 5:17).

Therefore, righteousness is not an intrinsic moral or religious state but rather the right or proper relationship to God established by God in Christ. So the question of whether people are really righteous or are only treated or accounted or reckoned as if they were righteous is a misunderstanding. Since righteousness is the right relationship with God which God has established in Christ, then people who by grace are drawn into this relationship are in fact actually righteous whatever their moral state. There is a righteousness based on the keeping of the law, which Paul himself had achieved (Phil. 3:6). This, however, is of no avail because it does not lead to the right relationship with God. Thus our righteousness depends entirely upon God, and our reliance upon God for this is faith. Therefore, says Paul, we are justified, made righteous on the basis of our faith (Rom. 3:28).

Now which of the above answers is most coherent with the biblical view of justification and righteousness? At first sight the first answer seems to be quite consistent with the biblical understanding. However, it implies by such terms as "accounted," "treats," and "imputed" that believers are dealt with by God as though they were righteous when in fact they are not. This in turn implies that righteousness is an intrinsic state, although this is denied in the latter part of the interpretation of the answer. In any case we have seen that righteousness is a relationship with God established by God in Christ and does not involve any "as if" situation.

The second answer seems more in line with this latter point in that the faithful are in fact righteous. However, the interpretation of this answer, in accordance with the traditional Catholic view, implies clearly that righteousness is an intrinsic state and that in justification the Christian is given this new condition. The Council of Trent declared that the condition or preparation for justification includes the presence of faith, hope, love, penitence, and the intention to receive baptism, begin a new life, and keep the commandments.[1] We have seen, however, that the consensus of the Bible is that it is precisely the sinners, the unrighteous, who are accepted by God as they are. In this answer justification is entirely by grace, but it is the justification of the righteous rather than the sinner.

This latter point, however, leads to a further difficulty in the first answer. Justification has an objective and a subjective aspect.[2] The objective aspect is the act of God in Christ restoring the covenant and opening it to all people. The subjective aspect is faith, trust in the divine factor, acceptance of the divine mercy. Apart from the presence of the subjective aspect there is no justification. People are not justified apart from their knowledge or against their will.

However, if we assert that the subjective aspect is necessary for justification, then we are claiming that those who are justified are in fact changed, different, brought into a new state or condition. If faith is a gift of grace or the Spirit, then it involves the divine presence in the believer. Faith as trust in the divine favor therefore involves hope in the divine mercy and the beginning at least of love of God and neighbor. This is the truth in the Catholic tradition and also the point at which the first answer is inadequate in that it apparently denies any change in the justified.

This leads to the third answer which can be interpreted to incorporate the positive points in the first two answers and to avoid their difficulties. In fact, as we have seen, the positive point of each answer is that it avoids the difficulty of the other. However, are the two positive points coherent? The points are that God forgives and accepts sinners as they are into the divine fellowship, and that these sinners are in fact changed by their trust in the divine mercy. These points are coherent because they are the two aspects of justification, the objective and the subjective, both of which are essential.

These points can be clarified by a personal analogy. A has offended against a personal relationship of deep friendship with B. A is helpless to restore the relationship. Nothing A can do is able to reestablish the friendship with B. What is necessary is that B should express pain and anger about A's action, forgive A, and offer to receive A back into fellowship. However, it is also necessary that A should believe in B, that is, trust B's sincerity, confess the offense, and accept B's forgiveness in order for the relationship to be reestablished. In this process the relationship is restored (A is accounted righteous, objective aspect) and A is changed (made righteous, subjective aspect).

Therefore, I conclude that the third answer is the correct one.

13

Election and Predestination

If God elects all people to salvation, can they all participate in salvation?

The significance of this question is that it raises the traditional problem of universalism, Will all people be saved?, and also that it points to one aspect of the current issue of religious pluralism, Can the adherents of other religions participate in salvation? The church in various periods has debated whether or not all people are elected to salvation, whether or not all people will be saved. During the past century as Christians came to realize that they were a decreasing minority in the world, the question of the relation of the universal claims of Christian faith to those of the other world religions has become more urgent. If only those who know God in Christ can be saved, is it possible that an increasing majority of humanity will not attain to salvation?

This question needs interpretation and focussing. I have argued in the text that God loves all people, wills that all be saved, and thus elects all people to salvation. The question focuses on whether and how the will of God can be fulfilled. Let us define salvation as comprehensive well-being based on communion with God through Christ by the Holy Spirit. Salvation can be interpreted historically, as taking place during earthly life, or eschatologically, in the final fulfillment. Let us limit the question to earthly historical life. Let us interpret "all" to refer to the dead, the living, and those yet to be born.

Within this interpretation of "all" we need to make another distinction between those who in their earthly lives hear the Christian gospel and respond in faith, those who hear and do not respond in faith, and those who do not hear. This distinction is, of course, not very clear. There are various degrees of hearing and responding, and all participation in salvation in earthly historical life is fragmentary (1 Cor. 13:12). Also the responsibility for this falls on the preacher as well as the hearer. The preaching of the church may involve the unnecessary stumbling blocks of fundamentalism, authoritarianism, moralism, obscurantism, and so forth, which make it impossible to be heard. (This is closely connected with the traditional doctrine of invincible ignorance that those who are ignorant of the gospel through no fault of their own are not guilty in God's eyes.)

The concept of participation in salvation also needs clarification. If we use the analogy of human personal relations, we can interpret salvation as entering a relation with God marked by openness, trust, and love. As there are degrees of intimacy and communion between persons, so there are degrees of intimacy and communion with God. Also since all human personal relations fall short of the ideal of perfect openness, intimacy, trust, and love, so also all human relations with God will fall short of the ideal described by Paul as "face to face" (1 Cor. 13:12) which will occur in the final fulfillment. So let us interpret participation in salvation to mean at least the beginning of the realization of the well-being based on a relation of communion with God marked by trust and love and established through Christ by the Holy Spirit.

Finally, the force of "can," that is, the nature and degree of this possibility, requires clarification. In this connection there are two kinds of possibilities, a possibility of principle and a possibility in fact. For example, it has always been a possibility in principle that people could fly to the moon, but only since 1969 has it been a possibility in fact. More to the point Romans 1:19-21 is sometimes interpreted to mean that while the gentiles have the possibility in principle of knowing God in a way sufficient for salvation, they do not have this possibility in fact, because they have lost it through sin.[1] Let us assume that the force of "can" in this question is that of a possibility in fact.

Because of these complications, let us limit the question and rephrase it as follows: Can those people who never hear the Christian gospel participate in salvation in their earthly lives?

The possible answers to this question are as follows:

1. No. They cannot participate in salvation.
2. They can participate partially in salvation.
3. Yes. They can participate in salvation.

Our procedure will be to explore the grounds for each of these answers in turn and then to determine which one is the most satisfactory.

1. No. They cannot participate in salvation. Throughout the Bible it is affirmed that salvation is offered only to those who consciously and explicitly repent and trust in God as God is manifest in the history of Israel culminating in Christ. Trust in other gods is denounced as idolatry which leads not to salvation but to destruction. Although at first the pagan gods are treated as real but inferior to the God of Israel, in the later prophets, however, they have no reality at all (Isa. 44:6-20). This theme culminates in such passages as John 14:6, "I am the way, the truth, and the life; no one comes to the Father but by me," and Acts 4:12, "And there is salvation in no one else, for there is no other name under heaven given among men by which we must be saved."

This answer is the only one which makes sense of the purpose of the church and its mission to the world. This mission which has a firm basis in the whole of the Bible is essentially that of proclaiming the love of God in the gospel of Christ to those who do not know God in Christ (Mt. 5:13-16, 28:18-20, 2 Cor. 5:18-20). If those who have never heard let alone re-sponded to the gospel of Christ can participate in salvation, then the mission of the church is entirely undercut and the central theme of the Bible is contradicted. It may be that those who have died will have another opportunity to hear and respond to the gospel, as is suggested in 1 Peter 3:20. The question, however, is concerned with earthly life, and on that the Bible is quite clear that there is salvation only in Christ. The consensus of the tradition is the same. In the form of the doctrine that there is no salvation outside the church, this was taught by Ignatius, Irenaeus, Clement, Origen, Cyprian, Augustine, the medieval schoolmen, and the Reformers, and it was made explicit in the Council of Florence in 1442.

If it is argued that all people can participate in Christian salvation through their own (non-Christian) religious traditions, then it must be pointed out that the interpretations of salvation in the various world religions are fundamentally different. Participation in Hindu or Buddhist salvation is essentially different from participation in Christian salvation. Presumably faithful Hindus and Buddhists participate in Hindu and Buddhist salvation, respectively, and this means precisely that they do not participate in Christian salvation. They do not want that. They want Moksha or Nirvana and not communion with God through Christ or the reign of God. So this argument can be made only out of ignorance of the world religions or on the basis of some theory that the essence of all religions is mysticism, for example.

2. They can participate partially in salvation. There are strands of tradition in the Bible which point toward a broader view of the possibility of salvation than that suggested above. All people are created in the image of God which means that they stand in a special relation of responsibility to God. All people also stand in a solidarity of sin, of having turned away from God in rebellion and disobedience. Thus all people stand under the grace and judgment of God who is the sovereign Lord of all nations (Amos 9:7). So the pagan nations and their rulers often appear as fulfilling the divine will in the judgment of Israel (Isa. 10:5-6). Furthermore, it is affirmed that God enters into a covenant with Noah and his descendants, that is, with all of humanity, a covenant involving the promise of God's favor as manifest in the order of nature (Gen. 8:21-9:17). Then within this universal covenant God establishes a special covenant with Israel as the divinely chosen people. This, however, does not involve a favored position for Israel but rather a special responsibility, namely, to bring God's blessing to all humanity (Gen. 12:1-3, Isa. 49:1-6). Thus the whole of human history becomes a history of salvation, of God seeking out all people to bring them to their fulfillment. Because of this all people stand in a

relation to God, and there is a suggestion in the Old Testament that even pagan religion can be a proper response to God (Mal. 1:11).

In the New Testament Jesus is presented as the fulfillment of the covenant with Israel which is intended for all humanity (Lk. 2:29-32). He knows little or nothing of pagan religion, but he continually rejects the nationalistic and exclusivistic attitudes toward the gentiles which he finds among some of his Jewish contemporaries. The gentiles will be judged on the same basis as the Jews and will share in the salvation of the final reign of God. Jesus even threatens the Jews that their place in the reign of God will be taken by the gentiles if they do not repent. He often points to the faith and love of gentiles as putting the Jews to shame (Mt. 8:5-13, 25:31-46, Lk. 10:29-37, 13:28-30, 17:11-19).

Paul condemns pagan religion as idolatry, but his point is that the gentiles are responsible for this, since they should have known better. They could and should have known God through the divine revelation in the creation and in their moral awareness, but they refused to acknowledge God and worshipped the creature rather than the creator (Rom. 1:18-21, 2:14-16). In the sermons put into the mouth of Paul in the Book of Acts he asserts that God is not left without a witness among the gentiles but has shown forth the divine goodness in the gifts of creation, is not far from anyone, and wants to be sought and found by everyone (Acts 14:15-17, 17:22-31). Finally, the author of the Fourth Gospel asserts that the active word or reason of God which was the divine agent in the creation of all the world is the light which enlightens everyone. Thus all people are related to God through their creation and illumination by the word of God (Jn. 1:1-9).

Drawing on this latter point the Christian apologists of the second century (and many later theologians) taught that the word or reason (*logos*) of God, since it was the divine agent in creation, is the pervasive principle of all reality. Humanity, which is created in the image of God, participates in the divine logos in human rationality. So all people have knowledge of God and of the divine will in varying degrees, but this knowledge is distorted by its partiality and by sin. Since the whole logos was incarnate and manifest in Christ, the more faithfully a person follows the leading of the logos the more closely does this person approximate to the Christian life. So even those who have no explicit knowledge of Christ can participate partially in Christian salvation.[2]

Thomas Aquinas, and most orthodox Catholic and Protestant theologians after him, taught that people can know a good deal about God and the divine will by the natural light of reason, namely, that God exists, is one and good, and is the creator and governor of the world. This makes it possible for one who follows this knowledge to participate partially in Christian salvation.[3] On the basis of these ideas later Christian thinkers have taught that all religions embody the essence of religion in varying degrees of perfection, but that the purest and fullest manifestation of the essence of religion has been manifest in Christianity. Others have taught that the religions of the world represent various stages in the progressive development of religion from its primitive forms to the great world religions of the present day, but that Christian faith is the highest stage of this development and the final form of religion. These constitute other ways of stating that the adherents of other religions participate partially in Christian salvation.

Therefore, since God is revealed to all people in the divine revelation in the creation and is present to all people through the divine presence in all of human history, all people have the opportunity and possibility of coming to know and trust God and to order their lives in accordance with the divine will. But since they lack the full revelation of God in Christ, they can participate only partially in Christian salvation.

If it is objected that because of sin and finitude Christians also can participate only partially in Christian salvation, then a distinction should be made between two kinds of partiality. If we take the analogy of human personal relations for salvation, then we can distinguish between an intimate adult personal relation, such as in marriage, and a relationship in which no words are spoken, in which there is no mutual self-disclosure through language, but only through gestures, as, for example, in the case of a parent and an infant. In both cases the relationships will fall short of the ideal of a fully open and intimate personal relation and thus will both be partial. In the latter case, however, a personal relationship has in fact been established, but it is limited in intimacy and mutual knowledge by the lack of verbal self-disclosure and thus will be partial in a different way.

A second analogy of these two types of partiality is the difference in the personal knowledge gained through the works of an artist and that gained through the artist's personal self-disclosure. In the first case there can be a sense of personal knowledge of the artist through a sympathetic and imaginative knowledge of the works, but this is limited by the lack of personal verbal self-disclosure. Again both kinds of knowledge of the artist will be partial, but their partiality is different. These analogies indicate the distinction between the kind of partiality involved in the Christian's participation in salvation and the kind of partiality involved in the participation in salvation of the adherents of other religions.

3. Yes. They can participate in salvation. If we assume that all participation in salvation during earthly life is partial and fragmentary, this answer means that there is no significant difference between the partial participation of Christians in salvation and the partial participation in salvation of those who never hear the gospel of Christ. The texts referred to in answer 1, namely, John 14:6 and Acts 4:12, assert that all salvation is through Christ, but they do not state that all salvation is only through explicit knowledge of Christ. The argument of answer 2 indicates that the

consensus of the biblical authors is that people can participate in salvation apart from explicit knowledge of Christ. God has planned and destined from the "foundation of the world" that all people should be saved through Christ (Eph. 1:3-10, Col. 1:15-20, 1 Pet. 1: 18-20). There are, however, millions who lived before Christ, and who live now and will live in the future without any explicit knowledge of Christ. If this is the case, then it must also be true that God can and will achieve the salvation of these people apart from explicit knowledge of Christ. This point is made by Karl Rahner in the following way:

> If, on the one hand, we conceive salvation as something specifically *Christian*, if there is no salvation apart from Christ, if according to Catholic teaching the supernatural divinization of mankind can never be replaced merely by goodwill on the part of man but is necessary as something itself given in this earthly life; and if, on the other hand, God has really, truly and seriously intended this salva-tion for all men—then these two aspects cannot be reconciled in any other way than by stating that every human being is really and truly exposed to the influence of divine, supernatural grace which offers an interior union with God and by mean of which God communicates himself whether the individual takes up an attitude of acceptance or of refusal towards this grace.[4]

If it is objected that this view undercuts the mission of the church, it can be stated in reply that God wills that implicit unreflective knowledge of God in Christ should be made explicit and reflected knowledge, because, all other things being equal, this offers a better chance of participating in salvation although not of a fuller participation. Furthermore, the preach-ing of the gospel of Christ can liberate the truth in the other religions from the errors with which it is connected and thus point the way to salvation more clearly.

If it is objected that Christian salvation is quite different from salvation in other world religions, it can be said in response that these differences should not be exaggerated. All religions attest the human awareness of alienation and bondage and the human need and longing for deliverance and healing, for fulfillment and salvation.[5] Through the working of divine grace the adherents of the other religions will be led to desire and hope for Christian salvation.

The God whom we know in Jesus Christ is not the kind of God who will hold it against people that, through no fault of their own, they do not know of Jesus Christ, but rather the God who loves all people equally and wills to bring all people to salvation through Christ. This is summed up finely in the Dogmatic Constitution on the Church of the second Vatican Council.

But if some men do not know the Father of our Lord Jesus Christ, yet acknowledge the Creator, or seek the unknown God in shadows and images, then God himself is not far from such men, since he gives life and inspiration to all (cf. Acts 17:25-28), and the Saviour wills that all men should be saved (cf. 1 Tim. 2:4). Those who, while guiltlessly ignorant of Christ's Gospel and of his Church, sincerely seek God and are brought by the influence of grace to perform his will as known by the dictates of conscience, can achieve eternal salvation. Nor does divine Providence deny the assistance necessary to salvation to those who, without having attained, through no fault of their own, to an explicit knowledge of God, are striving, not without divine grace, to lead a good life (II, 16).

Now which of these answers is the most satisfactory, that it, which one is supported by the strongest reasons or grounds and has made the most persuasive case? It seems that answer 1 has made the least persuasive case, so that the choice is between answers 2 and 3. Between these two it would seem that answer 2 has the greater weight of scripture and tradition on its side, and thus we must decide for this answer. People who never hear the Christian gospel can participate partially in Christian salvation in their earthly lives in a way different from that in which Christians participate partially in salvation. This difference is based on the advantage offered by explicit knowledge of God through Christ as explicated by the analogies given in answer 2.

14

Sanctification

What is the relation between sanctification and self-actualization?

The significance of this question is that it inquires about the relation between growth in the Christian life and growth as it is understood, for example, by humanistic psychology, one of the most influential contemporary schools of psychology. Sanctification is the main biblical and traditional term for the process and goal of the Christian life. Similarly self-actualization is one of the main contemporary psychological terms for the process and goal of human growth and development. For the person who is interested in both of these the question naturally arises about their relation. This question may also be important for one who wonders, for example, whether self-actualization is simply a modern scientific way of talking about a process which a pre-scientific age referred to as sanctification. As in the case of sin and neurosis this question is significant, because it is one specific and important instance of the general question of the relation of theological and psychological concepts.

As in the question on sin and neurosis we are investigating the relation of this phenomena by means of our inquiry about the relation of the concepts. Let as assume some working definitions of the key terms. Let us define sanctification as the process of becoming holy like God (Lev. 11:44, 1 Pet. 1:16) and Christ (Rom. 8:29, 2 Cor. 3:18) through the influence of the Holy Spirit, which is manifest in faith, hope, and especially love (1 Cor. 13). This process is also manifest in the other fruit of the Spirit: joy, peace, patience, kindness, goodness, faithfulness, gentleness, self-control (Gal. 5:22), and the other gifts of the Spirit: wisdom, knowledge, healing, miracles, prophecy, discernment, tongues, and interpretation (1 Cor. 12:8-10), and in service, contributing, giving aid, and acts of mercy (Rom. 12:6-8).

Let us define self-actualization, following Abraham H. Maslow, as the process of achieving psychological health variously described as self-fulfillment, emotional maturity, individuation, productiveness, authenticity, full-humanness, self-realization, and self-development. Maslow defines it "as ongoing actualization of potentials, capacities, and talents, as fulfillment of mission (or call, fate, destiny or vocation), as a fuller knowledge of, and acceptance of, the person's own intrinsic nature, as an unceasing trend toward unity, integration or synergy within the person."[1]

The characteristics of self-actualized people are

"superior perception of reality; increased acceptance of self, of others and of nature; increased spontaneity; increase in problem-centering [as against egocentering]; increased detachment and desire for privacy; increased autonomy, and resistance to enculturation; greater freshness of appreciation, and richness of emotional reaction; higher frequency of peak experiences; increased identification with the human species; changed (the clinician would say, improved) interpersonal relations; more democratic character structure; greatly increased creativeness; and certain changes in the value system."[2]

In another essay Maslow adds to this list the ability to discriminate between means and ends, between good and evil, and a philosophical unhostile sense of humor.[3]

The possible answers to this question are the logically possible relations between concepts. As we have seen above these are independence, contradiction, complementarity, identity, inclusion, and causality.[4] Our procedure will be to examine each of these possible answers in turn in order to determine which best describes the relation of sanctification and self-actualization.

Are the concepts independent, without significant relation? They might be considered to be independent if it were possible for a person at the same time to have maximal sanctification and minimal self-actualization or vice versa. However, since there is a considerable overlap in the content of the concepts, this would not be possible. Independence would also seem to be implied by the distinction of sanctification as supernatural in origin and self-actualization as natural. However, in view of the overlap it is conceivable that self-actualization could be understood to be a description of the human result of the influence of the Spirit of God. This would be a relation of causality or perhaps complementarity which would need to be explored before the concepts could be declared to be independent.

Are the concepts of sanctification and self-actualization contradictory or mutually exclusive such that if one is affirmed, the other must be denied? Because of the natural-supernatural distinction it might be concluded that if a particular characteristic or action of a person were the result of the influence of the Holy Spirit, then it could not be understood to be a result of natural human growth and development, and vice versa. If this were the case in regard to all the characteristics of sanctification and self-actualization, then the concepts would be contradictory.

In this connection it has been argued by F. B. Dilley and D. R. Griffin that any particular event cannot be at the same time the result of both divine and human action.[5] Yet as we saw in chapter 6 the testimony of the Bible and the tradition seems to point in another direction. In passages such as Galatians 2:20, 1 Corinthians 15:10, and Philippians 2:12-13 Paul implies that a fully human action can be at the same time a fully divine action. Aquinas and others have developed this idea in terms of the distinction between primary and secondary causes. God is the primary cause of all actions, but God in most cases acts through secondary causes such as the human will.[6] D. M. Baillie has developed this insight into a doctrine of the incarnation. Our experience of grace—I, yet not I—taken to the absolute degree is what incarnation is, namely, the identity of the fully divine and the fully human.[7] Therefore, I conclude that the concepts are not contradictory.

Are the concepts of sanctification and self-actualization complementary in the sense of being two aspects of one reality? This would mean that sanctification deals with a person's relation to God, while self-actualization deals with a person's inner dynamics and relations with other persons in the process of growth. The problem with this relation is that sanctification treats not only the relation to God, for example, in faith, but also inner dynamics and relations with other persons, for example, in love, joy, peace, patience, kindness, and service. In so far as both concepts describe psycho-social characteristics of people they are on the same level and cannot be considered to be complementary. However, to the degree that they do describe different dimensions of a process, they can be considered complementary. Besides faith other elements of sanctification deal with the relation to God. Peace is essentially peace with God (Rom. 5:1). Likewise hope, joy, wisdom, healing, prophecy, and tongues are concerned primarily with a person's relation to God. So I conclude that the relation of complementarity has a limited validity.

Are the concepts of sanctification and self-actualization identical? At first sight they seem to be quite distinct. Santification is the effect of the working of God the Holy Spirit on a person, whereas self-actualization is described as an entirely natural process. However, whereas the concepts may be distinct in regard to origin or cause, they may be identical in content. Although there is some overlap in the descriptions of the content of the concepts, there are also considerable areas which do not match. In particular faith and the various functions of service to the community listed in Romans 12:6-8 are absent or not stressed in the concept of self-actualization. Similarly the elements of creativity, fulfillment of potential, and some aspects of detachment and autonomy have no counterpart in the concept of sanctification.

Since Jesus is understood to be the fully sanctified person, one way to check whether the concepts are identical is to ask whether Jesus is also fully self-actualized. The New Testament authors are not interested in Jesus' personality, let alone his psychological make-up, but their writings do give indirectly a picture of some aspects of his character. When looked at in this way, Jesus does seem to fulfill most of the characteristics of the self-actualized person with a special emphasis on mission or vocation and compassion. However, there are some aspects of the picture of Jesus which are absent from the concept of self-actualization. The fundamental one is faith, complete trust in and obedience to God as the center of life and reality. This is central in the New Testament picture of Jesus and seems to be completely absent from the concept of self-actualization, except perhaps in the idea of the perception of and acceptance of reality.

Furthermore, there is an aura of elitism surrounding the self-actualized person which is totally absent from the picture of Jesus.[8] One aspect of this elitism is that Maslow states that self-actualization usually cannot even get under way until certain basic needs have been gratified, namely, physiological, safety, belongingness and love, and esteem needs. Furthermore the satisfaction of these needs has as its precondition various social freedoms and the freedom of the cognitive capacities. Needless to say these gratifications and preconditions are extremely rare in human history. In contrast the concept of sanctification was developed and lived out for centuries under conditions of a subsistence economy, social chaos, and political tyranny. Thus the self-actualized person is closer to the great-souled man of Aristotle than to Jesus or the saint of the Christian tradition.

This difference between the two concepts can be stated in another way. If the self-actualized person is seen to be seeking self-actualization, then the distinction between the two concepts may be seen to be fundamental in the light of one of Jesus' sayings: "If anyone would come after me, let him deny himself and take up his cross and follow me. For whoever would save his life will lose it, and whoever loses his life for my sake will find it" (Mt. 16:24-25). Thus between self-actualization and sanctification lies the necessity for conversion, for turning away from the self to God.[9] Given this fundamental difference, however, the partial identity of the concepts still holds.

Is the relation between these concepts one of inclusion, that is, is one included in the other as a member of a class? Self-actualization is never interpreted to include sanctification, but the reverse has been approximated. Theologians who tend to interpret theological concepts by means of psychological concepts have sometimes suggested that sanctification includes self-actualization. (See the discussion of Tillich below.) This is made possible by the overlap between the contents of the concepts and by the fact that sanctification is generally the more inclusive concept. However, we have noted that there are aspects of self-actualization which are not included in sanctification, such as the elements of creativity and the fulfillment of potential. So I conclude that the relation of inclusion has some limited validity.

Is the relation of the two concepts one of causality such that one is the cause of the other? Self-actualization could not be the cause of sanctification since it is not identical with the influence of the Holy Spirit which is the cause of sanctification, and also because it does not cause faith and the other aspects of sanctification involving the relation to God. Is sanctification the cause of self-actualization? This question could be interpreted in two ways. Does the process of sanctification cause the process of self-actualization? Does the influence of the Holy Spirit cause self-actualization? In so far as the concepts overlap in content, the first question is meaningless. So let us pursue the second question.

If the concept of self-actualization were defined in such a way as to rule out a supernatural cause, then the causal relation would not apply. However our provisional definition does not include this, and self-actualization is not usually so defined by psychologists. The causal relation would also be ruled out if sanctification were limited to members of the church. It was so limited by Calvin but not in the Bible and in other parts of the tradition. The prophets foresaw the day when the Spirit of God would be poured out on all people (Joel 2:28-29). The New Testament authors declared that the gentiles manifested some evidence of the working of the Holy Spirit. They had some knowledge of God and the law of God was written on their hearts (Rom. 1:19-20, 2:14-15). God is present to all people as creator, guide, judge, and savior (Acts 14:17, 17:25-31). Although the Christian tradition is not of one mind on this issue, the biblical view has become a consensus of contemporary theology.[10]

The only difficulty in the causal relation between the concepts is the lack of identity in their contents. It could be argued that the Holy Spirit is the cause of those elements in self-actualization which are included in sanctification. Or the concepts could be modified in ways which are coherent with their fundamental meaning and which would establish their identity in content.

An example of such modification is found in Paul Tillich's interpretation of sanctification in the third volume of his *Systematic Theology.* He defines it as "the life process under the impact of the Spiritual Presence" (229) which is his term for God the Holy Spirit. The Spiritual Presence is present to all people at all times (139). When the Spiritual Presence grasps people, their spirits are driven into self-transcendence or ecstasy, and the criterion of this is creativity (112, 120). The Spiritual Presence creates unambiguous life or fulfilled life but in a fragmentary way (112, 129, 140). This is manifest in faith and love. Formally faith is "the state of being grasped by that toward which self-transcendence aspires, the ultimate in being and meaning" (130). In this sense everyone has faith. The four principles which determine the character of sanctification are increasing awareness, increasing freedom, increasing relatedness, and increasing transcendence (231-37). In connection with relatedness Tillich states that "a decisive symptom of Spiritual maturity is the power to sustain solitude'' (234). Sanctification creates "a mature self-relatedness in which self-acceptance conquers both self-elevation and self-contempt in a process of reunion with one's self.'' This includes greater spontaneity, self-affirmation and vital self-expression (234-35, 240).

There is a remarkable congruity between Tillich's interpretation of sanctification and Maslow's view of self-actualization. However, there are distinct differences. Maslow ignores faith and tends to overlook the importance of the continuing destructive processes of psyche. Tillich does not stress the democratic values or identification with humanity. On the other hand Maslow does emphasize the importance of commitment to human values, and he concerned himself more and more with what he called the psychology of evil. Also Tillich in his other writings has emphasized the close relation of love and justice. In the light of all these considerations I conclude that the relation of causality has considerble validity.

In summary, we have found that the relations of the concepts of sanctification and self-actualization is one of partial identity, inclusion, complementarity, and more particularly causality. What is the significance of this conclusion? Looked at theologically self-actualization is human growth and development under the influence of the Holy Spirit. We saw in the text that various healing processes in human life and society can be understood theologically to be possible because they participate in God's universal healing activity.[11] In the same way we can understand the process of self-actualization, in so far as it is coherent with sanctification, to be the result of the influence of the Holy Spirit. The areas in which the two concepts do not overlap are the result of the differences between the naturalistic humanistic and the Christian theological perspectives which inform them. These differences appear especially in regard to faith and sin or the demonic-destructive element. Tillich describes the relation as follows:

> The image of perfection is the man who, on the battlefield between the divine and the demonic, prevails against the demonic, though fragmentarily and in anticipation. This is the experience in which the image of perfection under the impact of the Spiritual Presence transcends the humanistic ideal of perfection. It is not a negative attitude to human potentialities that produces the contrast but the awareness of the undecided struggle between the divine and the demonic in every man, which in humanism is replaced by the ideal of harmonious self-actualization. And it is the quest for the Spiritual Presence and the New Being as the conquest of the demonic that is lacking in the humanistic image of man and against which humanism rebels.[12]

15

History

Is there progress in history?

This question has been debated by philosophers and theologians throughout the modern period and especially in the last century. It has also been asked by innumerable people in the latter half of this century in the wake of two world wars, many other wars, seemingly endless social, economic, and political turmoil, and the threat of ecological disaster and total nuclear war. If there is no progress in any sense, then it is doubtful that there is any point in making the effort to improve things and that there is any meaning in history at all.

Is this a theological question? It may or may not be depending upon how it is interpreted. In order for it to be a theological question progress must be interpreted to refer to change in something in relation to God. This could be an increase in knowledge of God, love of God, communion with God, obedience to God, or in the fulfillment of the will of God. These can be summarized as the furthering of the purpose of God. "History" can refer to the history of the cosmos, the solar system, the earth, life, humanity, or some period or area of human history. Although some philosophers and theologians, such as Spencer and de Chardin, speak of progress in relation to cosmic and biological history, the usual referent of progress is human history.

Progress can be interpreted to be permanent or temporary. Permanent progress is progress which is not and cannot be lost, and it can refer to the whole life of a person, a nation, a civilization, or to the whole course of human history. Temporary progress can refer to any part of any of these. Let us assume that the question refers to permanent progress. There may be a sense in which there is progress which is temporary in history but permanent in relation to God.[1] However, since the question refers to progress in history, we shall limit it to that.

The prima facie reference of the question is broader than the life of an individual or a nation and could be a civilization or the whole of human history. So the question of permanence becomes an issue about the scope of the question. Since according to Toynbee there have been fourteen civilized and probably hundreds of so-called primitive societies which have ceased to exist, the question arises as to what permanence means in this connection. If there was a furthering of God's purpose in the history of a civilization which has died, this could be considered to be permanent beyond this civilization only if this furtherance were passed on in some way to a later civilization. Since this question is so complex and obscure, let us limit the scope of the question to the history of western civilization, which has become in some sense world-wide in our day, including the civilizations which are its direct parents, namely, the Hebraic, the Hellenic, and the Roman.

In summary the question can be rephrased as follows: Is God's purpose increasingly and permanently furthered in the history of western civilization?

There is an obvious temptation to treat the past aspect of the question as a historical one and to offer historical evidence for or against it. However, this is not a historical question but rather a theological one. Whether or not various historical figures believed that there had been or would be progress and whether or not certain events took place which might constitute progress as defined are historical questions. However, whether these people were correct and whether these events in fact constitute progress are theological questions.

Finally, we need to have a clearer idea of the nature of God's purpose in history. According to the Old Testament God's purpose in history is to bring salvation and peace to the whole creation through the calling of Israel (Isa. 9:2-7, 11:1-11, 49:6). In the New Testament this is focussed in and symbolized by Jesus Christ, in his teaching about the reign of God, and in his resurrection and the gift of the Spirit. The author of Ephesians refers to "the eternal purpose which God has realized in Christ Jesus our Lord," and "the purpose which God set forth in Christ as a plan for the fullness of time, to unite all things in him, things in heaven and things on earth" (3:11, 1:9-10). The purpose of God can also be stated in terms of the reign of God, the increase of the love of God and love of neighbor, the conforming of individuals and societies to the mind or spirit of Christ, and the humanization of society. These can be summarized in the statement that the purpose of God in history is to move the whole creation toward its fulfillment understood as perfect harmony and communion between God, humanity and nature.

Now what are the possible answers to this question? They are Yes, No, Yes and No, and indeterminate. Our procedure will be to investigate each answer in turn and then to determine which is the most satisfactory.

Yes. God's purpose is increasingly and permanently furthered in the history of western civilization. The grounds for this answer are found in many themes and passages of the Bible. According to the J and E authors God's purpose and promise in the calling of Abraham is that through him and his descendants all the families of the earth will be blessed (Gen. 12:2-

3). Israel is the light to the nations so that God's purpose and promise will reach all peoples (Isa. 49:6). The prophets announce the coming of a new age of peace and prosperity (Isa. 9:2-7, 11:1-9). Since God is the lord of history, the divine purpose and promise will be fulfilled (Isa. 51:4-6, 52:10). The coming of Jesus is the transformation of this promise and the beginning of its fulfillment.

In many of his parables Jesus taught that the reign of God, the rule of God in the world, is like leaven in meal, a mustard seed, and seed growing in a field. In the latter parable Jesus makes the point that the seed grows "of itself", *automate,* that is, automatically, spontaneously, apart from human agency (Mk. 4:26-29). These parables can be interpreted to mean that God's rule in the world grows secretly and steadily in human history.

The center of the teaching of the apostolic authors is that in the resurrection of Christ and the gift of the Spirit a new age of history has begun, the age of the church and its mission, and that in the preaching of the church all people are summoned to enter into this new age. God's purpose of bringing the message of salvation to all people will be fulfilled. "And this gospel of the kingdom will be preached throughout the whole world, as a testimony to all nations; and then the end will come" (Mt. 24:14; see 28:18-20, Mk. 13:10, Acts 1:8). Paul in particular foresees the world-wide success of the Christian mission in the time remaining (Rom. 11:25-26). Christian progress, however, is understood to be intensive as well as extensive. Christians individually and communally will be increasingly transformed by the Spirit of Christ (2 Cor. 3:18, Eph. 4:13-16), and this will have an impact on society and culture.

The earliest Christian confession was "Jesus is Lord." The risen Christ has all authority and power over all earthly powers and authorities (Mt. 28:18, Phil. 2:9-11, Col. 1:16, 2:10). Furthermore, Christ's rule in the world will be progressively increased until it is complete (1 Cor. 15: 25; see 2 Cor. 4:15). This will be the fulfillment of the plan and purpose of God from the beginning (Eph. 1:9-10, Col. 1:20). Historical evidence confirming this apostolic faith can be found in the spread of the Christian mission to all nations and the social and cultural impact of Christian faith in the increasing concern for the rights and integrity of the individual, and for justice, freedom, and equality. These biblical ideas of progress in history in the fulfillment of God's purpose for the creation appeared in the early Christian authors as the idea of the education of the human race toward spiritual maturity through the various stages of salvation history.[2] They came to the fore again in Calvinism, in the "fighting sects" of the seventeenth century, in the combination of these in English Puritanism, and in the liberal theology of the last century. All of these groups affirmed a dynamic hope for the progress of the reign of God in history.[3]

No. God's purpose is not increasingly and permanently furthered in the history of western civilization. The grounds for this answer are also found in many passages and themes of the Bible. The people of Israel were always unfaithful to covenant with God and to their calling to be a light to the nations (Jer. 8:4-6). The ambiguity of all human cultural achievements is depicted in the story of the tower of Babel (Gen. 11:1-9). If the reign of God is growing secretly, so also are the powers of evil, as in Jesus' parable of the tares (Mt. 13:24-30). The picture of the course of history which is given in the New Testament is one of the increasing power of evil, increasing tension, wars, famine, and persecution, all culminating in the return of Christ and the final judgment (Mt. 24, Mk. 13, Lk. 21, Rev. 6-9). There is a history of salvation events from the call of Abraham to the resurrection of Christ and the mission of the church, but there is no history of permanent progress in the human response of this in faith and love. The goal of history in the reign of God is not a matter of human achievement but of divine gift.

In Christian history there was no affirmation of the increasing and permanent furthering of God's purpose in history, apart from the epochal divine actions in salvation history, until the liberal theology of the last century. This theology of the steady increase of the reign of God in history was based on a faulty interpretation of Jesus' teaching. The work of Weiss and Schweitzer has undercut the biblical basis of this theology, and the history of this century has disproved it experientially.

In this century a majority of theologians had denied any permanent progress in human history.[4] Indeed many theologians have seen modern history as a story of regress rather than progress.[5] There may be temporary progress in the history of a person, a nation, or a civilization, but any such progress can be swept away by the tides of history. For example, much has been made of the progress of science and technology, but the actual history of technology has been a story of continual loss and reinvention.[6]

Yes and No. God's purpose is increasingly and permanently furthered in some areas of the history of western civilization and not in others. This answer combines elements of truth in the first two. There is permanent progress in the history of salvation, in the divine economy of preparation and fulfillment attested in the Bible and the mission of the church. In western history informed by the Bible there has been progress in knowledge of the creation, in technology or the means of human activity, in moral awareness, and in the possibilities for better social, economic, and political institutions. However, the human response to God's action in salvation history is always distorted by sin, and the human use of increasing knowledge and improving technology and institutions is likewise corrupted by estrangement from God.[7] There is in fact a spectrum of the areas in which progress is more or less possible. The farther an area of human activity is from that center of human life where we are concerned with the whole of human being and with the relation of humanity to God, the more progress is possible (logic, mathematics, natural science). The nearer we are to that center, the less is progress possible (morality, religion, philosophy, law).[8]

Indeterminate. God's purpose may or may not be increasingly and permanently furthered in the history of western civilization. Its possibility is affirmed in the positive answer, and its lack of necessity is affirmed in the negative answer. Its possibility cannot be denied, and its necessity cannot be affirmed. Since history is the realm of partial freedom, partial determination, and the freedom of divine grace, its course cannot be known to be progressive or non-progressive in the sense defined. The Christian affirmation of faith in the final victory of the divine purpose does not necessarily include its final victory in western history. There may have been progress in the past in western history, as is argued in the positive answer above, but any such progress may be lost in the future. Ecological disaster or total nuclear war could destroy all of humanity.

In conclusion, I believe that while there is some truth in the Yes and No answer in view of the permanence of the progress in the history of salvation, the indeterminate answer has the strongest claim to validity. The significance of this answer is that it leaves open the possibility of progress as defined as a motivation for human moral activity and responsibility.

16

Eschatology

What is the relation of Christian eschatology to the scientific picture of the future of the universe?

This question might arise for someone who has read about the death of the sun and the "heat death" of the universe and who wonders how these are related to the pictures of the end of the world in the Bible. Is the world going to end with the second coming of Christ or with increased radiation from the sun? Or is the latter really a modern scientific interpretation of what the former asserts in mythological form?

Eschatology is the doctrine of last things, the end of history and of the world. Since the question inquires about the scientific picture of the future of the physical world, let us focus our attention on what Christian eschatology says about that. The scientific picture of the future of the universe has been summarized in the text.[1] It involves the end of human life either through increased radiation from the sun or through the end of all such radiation. It also involves the heat death of the universe through the operation of the second law of thermodynamics resulting in the equalization of temperature and energy everywhere.[2]

What are the possible answers to this question, the possible relations between eschatology and science on the future of the physical world? They are identity or complementarity, independence, and contradiction.[3] Our procedure will be to explore each possible answer in turn and then to determine which one is the most satisfactory.

Identity or complementarity. What Christian eschatology says about the future of the physical universe is identical or complementary with what modern science says about this. This answer means that the scientific picture of the future of the physical universe is perfectly coherent with Christian eschatology, is identical with its assertions about the physical cosmos, and is complementary with its assertions about the relation of the cosmos to God. This relation has been possible, of course, only since the development of the modern scientific picture in this century. This view derives from the conviction that there is no conflict between theology and science, and that together they form a coherent world view. This is the view of contemporary liberal theology.

Tillich asserts that the scientific picture demythologizes or correctly interprets the apocalyptic symbolism of the end of the world. He avoids any contradiction with the scientific view by affirming a transition or elevation from the temporal to the eternal, an essentialization of the existential.[4] Gilkey following Whitehead argues that all of history and culture find their final completion and fulfillment by becoming part of the experience of God and by being maintained in the divine memory.[5] The grounds for these views are found mainly in idealist, existentialist, and process philosophy, although it is argued that they are the correct interpretation of the Bible and the tradition. The difficulty with this answer, besides the fact that its formulations are rather vague, is that the physical cosmos seems to be left out of the fulfillment or that its relation to the fulfillment is left unexplored.

Independence. There is no significant relation between what Christian eschatology and modern science say about the future of the physical universe. This is a radical form of the first answer and is represented by existentialist theology and especially by Bultmann. Here Christian faith and theology are understood to be concerned only with human consciousness or human existence and in no sense with the physical cosmos. The doctrines of creation, providence, incarnation, and resurrection are interpreted in such a way as to have no connection with or implication for physical reality. Therefore, questions about the future of the cosmos are not considered to be theological questions.

For Bultmann the New Testament assertions about the transformation of the cosmos are interpreted to mean that in the cross of Christ and in its preaching the world and its claims have come to an end for Christians and thus they are free from the world. According to Bultmann this kind of demythologizing interpretation was begun by Paul (Gal. 6:14-15, 1 Cor. 3:21-23, 7:17-24, 29-31, 9:19-23). It was carried further by the Johannine author for whom the second coming, the last judgment, and the resurrection have already occurred for believers in the appearance and preaching of Jesus (Jn. 3:18-19, 5:24, 9:39, 11:25-26, 12:31). Therefore, for Bultmann eschatology has no future reference except in the sense of the next moment of human existence, and it has no reference at all to the physical cosmos.

This is a possible interpretation of the New Testament, and it has been argued ably by Bultmann and his followers. It had little support in the tradition until the liberal theology of the last century. Its main problem is that it does not do justice to the significance of the physical world and its fulfillment which is attested throughout the Bible and the tradition.

Contradiction. Christian eschatology contradicts the scientific picture of the future of the physical universe. This answer is the prima facie meaning of the Bible and the tradition, although of course they did not know of the modern scientific picture. The Old Testament authors attest the transformation of the natural world, the earth, plants and animals, in connection with the regeneration of Israel (Isa. 11:6-9, 35:1-7, 43:19-20, 51:6, 65:17, 66:22). In the New Testament almost every author asserts that at the end of history heaven and earth will pass away or be transformed and a new heaven and earth will appear (Mk. 13:24-25, 31 par, Mt. 5:18. 1 Cor. 7:31, 2, Pet. 3:10-13, Rev. 21:1-5). According to Paul the creation will be delivered from bondage into liberty (Rom. 8:19-22). This transformation of the creation is understood on the model of the transformation of the Christian who is seen as a new creation (2 Cor. 5:17, Gal. 6:15), and as a first fruits of the consummation of the world (Jas. 1:18).

This view of the future of the universe was generally affirmed in the tradition down to the liberal theology of the last century.[6] In the liberal theology, however, eschatology is historicized, and the idea of the transformation of the world disappears. In this century the neo-orthodox theology of Barth and Brunner and the eschatological theology of Moltmann and Pannenberg have strongly reaffirmed the doctrine of the transformation of the cosmos.[7] The evolutionary theology of de Chardin also gives this answer to the question. His concepts of radial energy and the Omega point constitute a contradiction of the scientific idea of heat death through increase of entropy.[8] He accepts the end of life on earth but affirms a mystical escape.[9]

The primary reason for accepting this answer is its solid basis in the Bible and the tradition. Its main difficulty is its conflict with modern science. I have argued in the text that there is no conflict between science, especially natural science, and theology, and that any apparent conflict is either a theological or a scientific error. This applies especially to the relation of theology to scientific assertions about the present structures and processes of the world. It also applies to scientific assertions about the history of the cosmos.[10] What about scientific predictions about the future of the cosmos? Such predictions assume the continuity of the basic framework of physical reality as elaborated by modern physics and astronomy, and there is no way of proving this assumption. Furthermore, from a theological point of view the "basic framework" of all reality is God as creator, lord, and redeemer, who is free to fulfill the divine purpose in the creation. The will and purpose of God is the foundation of the basic framework of physical reality and they are unchanging. Any changes in the subordinate orders of the framework of physical reality are in accordance with this unchanging purpose. Therefore, it can be argued that the transformation and fulfillment of the cosmos do not constitute a conflict with science but only with the interpretation of science in some world view such as naturalism.

Thus I conclude that the third answer has the best claim to validity, namely, that Christian eschatology contradicts the scientific picture of the future of the physical universe.

17

Church

Which is more important in the mission of the church, evangelism or service?

This is a question which has always concerned the church and especially in the modern period. It still often divides congregations and churches, especially evangelical and liberal churches. The question concerns priorities in the purpose or reason for being of the church. Thus it affects practical decisions in the allocation of resources in the work of the church.[1]

By "evangelism" let us understand the explicit proclamation of the gospel in formal and informal settings directed primarily to those who are not active members of the church. Let us interpret "service" broadly to include all types of activity born of Christian love to help those in need, both social service and social and political action. The "mission of the church" can be interpreted narrowly or broadly, and the answer to the question may vary accordingly. It can be understood to refer to the overall purpose or reason for being of the church or more specifically to its responsibility for preaching the gospel. Since the latter interpretation would amount to a resolution of the question by definition, let us use the former interpretation.

It is important to note the limitation of the question to the mission of the church broadly interpreted. If it referred to the Christian life, the answer might be different. The reason is that the purview of the doctrine of the church is not identical with that of the Christian life. The former is focussed on the community and the latter on the individual. Thus it might possibly be argued that evangelism is more important in the purpose of the church, whereas service is more important in the Christian life.

"More important" can mean a variety of things: of higher priority, of greater urgency, having a stronger claim on the resources of the church, of greater significance in or involving a fuller manifestation of the mission of the church, or more essential to the mission of the church. Let us choose the last meaning, since it is the most fundamental in the sense that the others could be dependent upon it. However, it requires further clarification.

"Essential" means necessary to the being of something. In our question it means that without which the mission of the church could not be what it is supposed to be. A weaker meaning is "necessary to the fullness of the being" of something. In these two levels of essentiality there can be a more or less only on the second level. Thus "more essential" means more necessary to the fullness of being of the mission of the church. However, it does not mean that the church should always expend more of its resources on the element so described, that this element should always have temporal precedence, or that it is always more urgent than the other. Decisions about this will always depend upon the circumstances and especially the situation and needs of the people involved and the resources of the church.

Let us use an analogy. It can be argued that in the parent-child relationship the parental expression of love and affection is more essential to the well-being of the child than the parental satisfaction of the physical needs of the child, although the former can be expressed through the latter. This does not mean that the parental expression of love is always more urgent, should always claim more parental time and energy, or should always precede the parental satisfaction of physical needs. These things will always depend upon the circumstances.

Now the question can be rephrased: Which is more necessary to the fullness of being of the purpose of the church, evangelism or service? The possible answers to this question are that evangelism is more necessary that service, that service is more necessary than evangelism, and that evangelism and service are equally necessary to the fullness of being of the purpose of the church. Our procedure will be to explore each of these answers and then to determine which is most satisfactory.

1. Evangelism is more necessary than service to the fullness of being of the purpose of the church. The necessity of the proclamation of the good news of God's love is fundamental throughout the Bible. It has its roots in the prophetic announcement of the coming of God's salvation (Isa. 40:9, 41:27, 52:7). It is focussed in Jesus' preaching of the arrival of the reign of God (Mk. 1:15, Lk. 4:18, quoting Isa. 61:1) which was the main purpose of Jesus' ministry. The gospel of Mark records that when Jesus' disciples came to him saying that everyone was looking for him, presumably to have him heal their sick, he responded, "Let us go on to the next towns, so that I may preach there also; for that is why I came out" (Mk. 1:38). Jesus sent his disciples out to proclaim the nearness of the reign of God (Mt. 10:7, Lk. 9:2, 10:1-9). The risen Christ sent out the apostles to preach the gospel to all nations (Mt. 24:14, 28:19, Mk. 13:10, Lk. 24:47, Acts 1:8). Paul understands preaching to be his main responsibility (1 Cor. 1:17, 9:16). The reason for this is that this is the only way the faith

can be spread (Rom. 10:14, 1 Cor. 1:21). The Book of Acts is the story of the missionary expansion of the church through the preaching of the gospel. This is the beginning of the fulfillment of the plan and purpose of God from the beginning to bring the whole creation to its fulfillment through Christ (Eph. 1:9-10, 3:8-11). The proclamation of the gospel has been understood to be the heart of the purpose of the church down through Christian history. This has been seen more closely in some periods than in others, but it came to clear expression and enactment in the great missionary expansion of the church in the modern period.

2. Service is more necessary than evangelism to the fullness of the being of the purpose of the church. The Christian vocation to service or servanthood is based on the prophetic calling of the people of Israel to be the servant of God who is to bring justice to the nation and to suffer for the sins of the world (Isa. 42:1-4, 53:4-6). Reflecting this tradition Jesus says that he came not to be served but to serve (Mk. 9:35, Lk. 22:27). Therefore he is called the servant of God (Acts 3:13, 26, 4:27, Rom. 15:8, Phil. 2:7). The essential element in discipleship to Jesus, in contrast to the way of the world, is service of others. This is stressed repeatedly in the gospels (Mt. 23:2-12, Mk. 9:33-35, 10:42-45, Lk. 22:24-27, Jn. 12:12-17). When Jesus called the twelve, the authority he gave them was over unclean spirits and to heal diseases, rather than to preach the gospel (Mt. 10:1, Mk. 6:7, Lk. 9:1).

In imitation of Christ Christians are called to be the servants of others in love (Gal. 5:13). The love of God and the love of neighbor are the essence of the Old Testament law (Mk. 12:31 par). Therefore love is the fulfilling of the law (Rom. 13:9, Gal. 5:14). In fact love is greater than faith and hope and is the sine qua non of all human abilities and actions (1 Cor. 13). In the final judgment our lives will be assessed as to whether we have served those in need, that is, fed the hungry, given drink to the thirsty, welcomed the stranger, clothed the naked, visited the sick and those in prison, and not whether we have evangelized them (Mt. 25:31-46).

Therefore the highest requirement of the mission of the church is loving service, whole-hearted concern for the well-being of those in need. This is summarized in a study by the World Council of Churches in the following way: "The Church exists for the world. It is called to the service of mankind, of the world. This is not election to privilege but to serving engagement."[2]

3. Evangelism and service are equally necessary to the fullness of being of the purpose of the church. There is an equal stress throughout the Bible on the necessity of the proclamation of God's salvation and the call to serve those in need. The prophetic denunciation of oppression of the poor and helpless and the call to care for those in need are always found side by side with the prophetic announcement of the coming of salvation. The

prophets proclaimed the coming day of the lord and the messianic age and announced that the signs of this coming would be that the sick will be healed, justice done, the poor no longer oppressed, the hungry fed, and the naked clothed (Isa. 11:4-5, 29:18-21, 35:3-6, 58:6-12, 61:1-3).

Throughout his ministry Jesus both preached and healed and fed the hungry. When the disciples of John the Baptist were sent to Jesus to ask whether he was the one who is to come, Jesus answered them: "Go and tell John what you hear and see: the blind receive their sight and the lame walk, lepers are cleansed and the deaf hear, and the dead are raised up, and the poor have good news preached to them" (Mt. 11:4-6; see Lk. 7:22). When Jesus sent out the twelve, his instructions were both to preach the reign of God and heal the sick (Mt. 10:7, Mk. 3:14, Lk. 9:2, 10:9). Likewise the apostles healed as well as preached (Acts 3). The church in Antioch organized relief for those suffering from famine in Judea (Acts 11:27-30). Paul was greatly concerned to aid the poor (Gal. 2:10) and especially to make a collection from all the churches he visited to help the needy in Jerusalem (Rom. 15:25-31, 1 Cor. 16:1-4, 2 Cor. 8, 9), as well as to preach the gospel.

Throughout its history the church has been concerned equally with evangelism and service of those in need, and the reason for this is clear. Christian salvation is best understood as wholeness or well-being in the most comprehensive sense, including physical, psychological, social, economic, and political well-being, as well as spiritual well-being. Therefore, the preaching of the gospel of salvation in this comprehensive sense will always be accompanied by signs of this new reality in the form of service of those in need.

On the whole, the first two answers seem to be one-sided in opposite ways, and the third answer seems to combine their strong points. Therefore, I conclude that evangelism and service are equally necessary to the fullness of being of the purpose of the church.

18

Sacraments

What happens between God and the recipient in baptism?

Church people often wonder what is really going on in baptism. Is it a quasi-magical rite which accomplishes something simply in the doing of it which could not be achieved in any other way? Or is it essentially a social rite of initiation into an institution like a fraternity initiation? The mysterious language of the service sounds like the former, but baptism is often understood simply as the latter. So this question makes explicit the inarticulate wonderings of many people in the church. To be sure it reflects the point of view of modern individualism and implies a lack of awareness of the biblical and traditional Christian view that God is related primarily to the community of faith and only to the individual as a member of the community. In this latter context, however, it is an an important question.

I interpret the question to be inquiring about a possible change in the relation between God and the recipient in baptism or about God doing something or giving something in baptism which is not given or done apart from it. Since baptism normally occurs in the context of the ministry of the word and the eucharist,[1] it needs to be made clear whether the question is asking about what happens in the whole service or only in the washing with water in the triune name of God. Let us assume that the question is inquiring about what happens between God and the recipient in the washing with water in the context of the whole service including the ministry of the word and the eucharist.

In order to avoid the issues associated with infant baptism, let us assume that the candidate is an adult. Let us also assume that the candidate fulfills the conditions for baptism, namely, repentance, renunciation of evil, faith in Christ, and the promise of obedience. I interpret this to mean that the candidate has heard the gospel, has responded in faith, has been instructed, attends public worship with the exception of the sacraments, and engages in private prayer.

Now what is happening between God and the candidate before baptism? God is present to the candidate as creator and sustainer. God is present as lord, judge, and savior in all the candidate's experience. God is revealed to the candidate through Christ by the Spirit, especially in preaching and the reading of the Bible and prayer. God offers the divine presence to the candidate in salvation and the gifts of the Spirit, all in the context of the community of faith, the church. Also the candidate has responded in faith to God's presence in salvation and the gifts of the Spirit to some degree. The degree of this participation is one way of putting the point of the question. Now this may seem to be a very large assumption, but it is the normal expectation of adult candidates for baptism from New Testament times to the present.

What are the possible answers to this question?

1. Nothing new happens between God and the recipient in baptism.

2. In baptism God gives the forgiveness of sin, the Holy Spirit, and membership in the church.

3. Various things may happen between God and the recipient in baptism. Our procedure will be to investigate the grounds for each of these possible answers and then to determine which is the most coherent with the Bible and the tradition.

1. Nothing new happens between God and the recipient in baptism. There is no change in the relationship. God does not do or give anything which was not done or given already. Thus baptism is essentially a public declaration of the recipient's faith and initiation into the church, a making de jure of something which is already present de facto. A change may occur in the recipient through the psychological impact of the solemn act of public commitment and initiation into the community, but nothing new happens between God and the recipient.

The story of Pentecost in Acts 2 indicates that the gift of the Spirit to the apostles (and the others) preceded their baptism, if they were in fact ever baptized. When Peter preached to Cornelius and his household, the Holy Spirit came upon them, and Peter asked, "Can anyone forbid water for baptizing these people who have received the Holy Spirit just as we have?" (Acts 10:47).

Although the tradition of the church came to affirm that forgiveness of sin, the Spirit, and membership in the church were given only in baptism, the practice of the church contradicted this. The period of instruction and probation came to extend as long as two years during which the candidate participated in the life of the church with the exception of the sacraments. As conditions of baptism the church required repentance, renunciation of evil, confession of faith, and the promise of obedience. However, these are all gifts of the Holy Spirit, the fruit of the presence of God to the candidate (Acts 5:31, 11:18, 1 Cor. 12:3, 2 Tim. 2:25). These conditions were reaffirmed in the tradition of the church. The catholic tradition is summarized, for example, in the Council of Trent, where the conditions required for baptism include faith, belief in the gospel, hope in God, repentance, intention to begin a new life and keep the commandments of God, all of which are gifts of the Spirit.[2]

Thus baptism is essentially a public declaration of what has happened, continues to happen, and will happen between God and the recipient in the community of faith. Such a declaration is very important in the Christian life. As is the case in the declaration of human love, so the declaration of the divine love in baptism confirms it, enhances it, and more fully elicits the response of the recipient. However, nothing new happens between God and the recipient in baptism.

2. In baptism God gives to the recipient the forgiveness of sin, the Holy Spirit, and membership in the church. This is the clear teaching of the New Testament. Christian baptism is modeled on that of John the Baptist and his baptism of Jesus. John says that Jesus will baptize with the Holy Spirit (Mk. 1:8, par, Jn. 1:33, Acts 1:5, 11:16), and Jesus' baptism by John involves the gift of the Spirit (Mk. 1:10 par). According to the Book of Acts baptism accomplishes the forgiveness of sin and the gift of the Spirit (2:38). Sometimes the Spirit is given in connection with the laying on of hands which is the completion of the baptismal initiation (Acts 8:14-17, 19:6).

Paul's teaching is that baptism includes the gift of the Spirit and incorporation into the church (1 Cor. 12:13). He interprets baptism as a putting on of Christ or an identification with Christ in his death and resurrection which involves the forgiveness of sin and new life (Rom. 6:3-11, Gal. 3:27, Col. 2:12f; see 1 Pet. 3:21). John associates baptism with the gift of the Spirit and rebirth (Jn. 3:5; see Titus 3:5).

Toward the end of the second century Tertullian summarized the teaching of the church on what happens in baptism, and nothing essential has been added to his statement since then. According to him baptism accomplishes the remission of sins, deliverance from death, regeneration, the bestowal of the Holy Spirit, and by implication membership in the church.[3]

This interpretation of what happens between God and the recipient in baptism involves an action or gift of God in response to or on the condition of a human action. This pattern can be seen in Jesus' teaching and ministry. In his teaching about prayer the point of the stories about the importunate friend, the son who asks his father for a fish, and the importunate widow and the judge is summarized in the saying, "Ask, and it will be given you; seek, and you will find; knock, and it will be opened" (Lk. 11:9; see 18:1-8). Sometimes in the accounts of his healing Jesus requires the person to ask for what is desired (Mk. 10:51 par).

3. Various things may happen between God and the recipient in baptism. Baptism is the symbol of the whole process of initiation into the Christian life in the church. Any element in this process or none of them may occur during the actual rite.

From the New Testament we get a picture of the process of initiation into the church which includes various elements: hearing the gospel, conversion or the decision of faith, repentance and amendment of life, instruction, reception of the Spirit, and participation in the eucharist and the Christian community life. (See, for example, Acts 2:37-47, 9:1-19.) These elements may occur in different orders. Baptism may occur at various points in this process, normally after hearing the gospel, the decision of faith and repentance, sometimes before the gift of the Spirit, as in Jesus' baptism (Acts 2:38, 8:14-17, 19:5-6), and sometimes after (Acts 2, 10:44-48). When infant baptism developed, it obviously occurred before all of these elements.

It has also been the case down through Christian history that the various elements in the process of Christian initiation have occurred in different orders and that baptism has occurred at various points in this process. For example, in the case of Augustine baptism took place after instruction and conversion; in the case of John Wesley it took place before these.

The process of Christian initiation is one of God being made known more and more fully to the person, giving the divine presence more fully, moving the person to repentance and faith, drawing the person into communion and into the life of the Christian community. The relation of baptism to this process can be understood on the analogy of the relation of the marriage service to the process of a couple coming to know one another. In some cultures and periods the marriage ceremony takes place at the very beginning of the relationship. In other cultures and periods it takes place after the couple has been married de facto for some time. Likewise baptism represents the whole process of Christian initiation, can occur at any point in it, and can be accompanied by any element in the process. The principle is that the Spirit like the wind is beyond human comprehension and control; it blows where it wills (Jn. 3:8).

The institutional church was made rather uneasy by this divine unpredictability and understandably tried to pin down certain elements of the process of initiation. The Council of Trent declared that the sacraments confer grace simply by being performed, *ex opere operato*. Since baptism represents the whole process, this was not an error. Yet it cannot be asserted that particular elements in the process occur only in the actual rite of baptism.

Now which of these answers is most coherent with the consensus of the biblical authors as interpreted in the tradition? The third answer seems to be most coherent with the Bible, but the second is clearly most in accord with the tradition. In such cases of conflict, we must side with the Bible. Furthermore, the third answer is also a possible reinterpretation of the tradition. Therefore I conclude that the third answer is the most valid.

19

Worship

Is corporate worship essential to the church?

The Christian churches probably expend well over half of their resources on corporate worship. This is in the form of buildings and their maintenance, support of organists, choirs, and clergy, most of whom spend a large amount of their time in planning and conducting corporate worship. Therefore the churches ought to be very clear about their rationale for corporate worship, why it is necessary. However, most church teaching about worship assumes this and discusses other matters about worship. Moreover, as indicated in the text,[1] some common rationales for worship are not coherent with the teaching of the Bible. So this question raises a most important issue for the churches. It also treats indirectly a question which is fundamental for the Christian life. Many Christians wonder whether or not attendance at corporate worship is essential to the Christian life.

Let us understand "corporate worship" to refer to the gathering of Christians beyond the individual family for the purpose of praise, thanks, confession, intercession, hearing the word, and sacramental celebration. Thus any eucharist or baptism will be corporate. Let us interpret "essential" to mean necessary to the being of the church, that without which the church would not be the church. Since corporate worship is not continuous but rather occasional although regular, essential here means necessary to the being of the church in the long run. That is, if corporate worship is essential to the church, and if it ceased today, the church would not cease to exist tomorrow but rather in a matter of months or years. There is a weaker meaning of essential which means necessary for the well-being or the fullness of being of something.

Finally, let us interpret "church" to refer to the human community which is affirmed in the creeds as one, holy, catholic, and apostolic, and in the New Testament as the congregation of the faithful, the body of Christ, the fellowship of the Holy Spirit, the community of hope, and the people of God. Thus necessary to the being of the church means necessary to the existence of this community. It is conceivable that an institution could continue to exist which had ceased to be the church.

What are the possible answers to this question? They are as follows:

1. Yes. Corporate worship is essential to the being as well as to the well-being and the fullness of being of the church.

2. Corporate worship is not essential to the being of the church, but it is essential to the well-being and fullness of being of the church.

3. No. Corporate worship is essential neither to the being nor to the well-being or fullness of being of the church.

Our procedure in this question will be to explore the New Testament and the tradition on this issue and then to determine which of the possible answers best fits the evidence.

Although Jesus and his disciples apparently attended the synagogue and occasionally the temple, Jesus' interpretation of God's command included nothing about corporate worship. No New Testament author asserts explicitly that corporate worship is essential to the being of the church, but they all probably assume that Christians always have and always will participate in corporate worship, especially the eucharist (Acts 2:42, 46, 20:7, 1 Cor. 1:16-17, 11:17-20, 33, Eph. 5:18-20, Heb. 10:25). The closest that any New Testament author comes to affirming the essentiality of corporate worship is Paul's discussion of the church as the body of Christ (1 Cor. 12:12-31, Rom. 12:4-8). The members of the church are seen as members of a body which have different functions, are interdependent, and care for one another. What makes the church one body is participation in the Spirit of Christ through baptism and in the body of Christ in the eucharist. "By one Spirit we were all baptized into one body—Jews or Greeks, slaves or free—and all were made to drink of one Spirit." "The bread which we break, is it not a participation in the body of Christ? Because there is one loaf, we who are many are one body, for we all partake of the same loaf" (1 Cor. 12:13, 11:16-17). This it is through corporate worship in baptism and the eucharist that the church realizes itself as the one body of Christ.

Early church authors asserted or assumed the regular and universal celebration of the eucharist.[2] During the medieval period the eucharist was described as the supreme sacrament and essential to the Christian life in the church. The Augsburg Confession and the Anglican Articles of Religion defined the church in terms of the presence of the word of God and the two gospel sacraments. The Anglican catechism describes these sacraments, baptism and the eucharist, as "generally [that is, universally] necessary to salvation." There were occasions in the history of the church when corporate worship was infrequent, for example, in periods of severe persecution and among the hermits of the early medieval periods. However, most of the hermits gathered monthly for corporate worship, and even during extreme persecution the fact that Christians managed to gather secretly indicates the intensity of their commitment to the necessity of corporate worship.[3]

Now which of these possible answers is supported by the evidence from the Bible and the tradition? First of all the evidence eliminates the third answer. Although the essentiality of corporate worship is not explicitly asserted in the New Testament, it is asserted early and universally in the tradition. Also the universal presence of corporate worship from the very beginning attests this essentiality at least in the sense of being necessary for the well-being and the fullness of being of the church. So our choice is between the first two answers.

Since the first two answers agree on this latter point, they must be compared on the issue of whether or not corporate worship is essential in the strict sense. In support of the second answer it can be argued that the essentiality of corporate worship is nowhere asserted in the New Testament. However, the corporate nature of the church is affirmed there, and this implies the necessity for the gathering of the church. The continued existence of a community requires that it realize itself as a community through mutual knowledge and activity, and this requires regular gathering. However this gathering need not take the form of corporate worship. It can be for the purpose of fellowship, study, mutual help, and the administration of the community. Prayer is essential to the Christian life in the church, but it can be done privately and in families. Thus it can be argued that corporate worship is not essential to the being of the church.

In support of the first answer it can be argued that although the essentiality of corporate worship is not explicitly asserted in the New Testament, it is clearly implicit and is made explicit very early and universally in the tradition. So this issue does not constitute a contradiction between the Bible and the tradition but rather a relation of implicit and explicit. Furthermore, the New Testament authors clearly assert the corporate nature of the church, and this is most immediately and naturally realized and manifest in corporate worship. The idea of gathering for all purposes except that of worship would be an anomaly. Finally, we have the testimony of Paul noted above that it is through baptism and the eucharist that the church is constituted as the fellowship of the Spirit and the body of Christ.

Therefore, I conclude that the first answer is correct, and that corporate worship is essential to the being of the church.

20

Ministry

Is there a theological difference between a lay person and an ordained person?

There has been a great deal of discussion recently about the meaning of ordination, the ministry of the laity, and the relation of lay and ordained ministry in the church. Arguments on these issues are often based on an affirmation or denial of the unique status of the clergy. The above question deals with an issue which underlies many of these debates, and a resolution of it would move the discussion forward. Thus it seems to be a significant question whose resolution might have important practical results.[1] For example, if we conclude that there is a theological difference between lay and ordained persons, it could be argued that clergy should have more say in the government of the church or greater advantages or benefits in church and society, and vice versa.

The key concept needing clarification is that of a theological difference. Since theology concerns God and the world in relation to God, a theological difference would be a difference in the relation to God. Now it might be argued that since each person is unique, he or she stands in a unique relation to God which is different from that of any other person. Thus there is a theological difference between any two persons, including lay and ordained persons. However, I interpret the question to refer to differences in relation to God growing out of the presence of ordination and not simply out of the uniqueness of persons.

Now if we can understand a person's relation to God on the analogy of the relations between persons, then differences in relation to God will be analogous to differences in the relations between persons. The relation between God and persons has been understood on the analogy of the relations of parent and child, monarch and subject, spouses, teacher and pupil, and on the analogy of human love, estrangement, fear, adoration, loyalty, intimacy, and anger. Thus a difference in relation to God understood on the analogy with any of these differences would be a theological difference.

In order to clarify further the concept of a theological difference, let us examine some specific examples of such differences. A model case would be that of the difference in relation to God between Jesus and other people. In the New Testament the relation between Jesus and God is understood on the analogy of an intimate relation of trust and love between a father and a son. Other people are called by Jesus into a similar relation to God, but a relation which is different in being not as intimate or special and in being based on Jesus' relation to God. The tradition made this difference more definite by asserting that Jesus was fully divine and that God the Son is incarnate in Jesus.

Another model case of a theological difference would be that between a faithful Christian and a person who denies God, Christ, and the gospel. Both stand in the same relation to God in being creatures of God, sinners, loved by God, and having the potentiality of salvation or communion with God. However the faithful Christian participates in these relations consciously and therefore more fully and in the actuality of salvation or communion with God, and the denier of God does not. This amounts to a difference in relation to God and thus a theological difference.

Since ordination is a sacramental act, we can consider the related case of the difference in relation to God between a person who is baptized and one who is ready and desirous of baptism but not yet baptized. According to the conclusion of chapter 18 there is a difference in relation to God between one who has not yet begun the process of Christian initiation and one who has completed it. However, since baptism may occur at any point in this process, there may or may not be a theological difference between these two people. But according to the tradition baptism mediates the forgiveness of sin, the gift of the Holy Spirit, and membership in the church, and this would involve a difference in relation to God and thus a theological difference.

Now the possible answers to this question are obviously Yes and No. Our procedure will be to investigate the case for each answer in turn and then to assess which has the greatest support in the Bible and the tradition.

Yes. There is a theological difference between a lay person and an ordained person in the sense of a difference in their relation to God. Three grounds can be given for this: a special inner call by God, a special gift of grace, and a unique character and ontological status.

To be specially called by God is to stand in the tradition of the prophets, Jesus, and the apostles. God called the prophets to speak the divine word to the people (Isa. 6, Jer. 1:4-10, Amos 7:14f). Jesus called the twelve apostles and sent them out to preach and heal (Mk. 6:7 par, 3:13-19 par). The Holy Spirit calls Paul and Barnabas to their missionary work (Acts 13:2). The apostles were the foundation and origin of the later ordained ministry of the church. Summarizing this tradition the Anglican ordinals since the sixteenth century have included the questioning of the candidates as to whether they believe that they have been truly called by God to the order in question.

Ordination in the Bible and the tradition is also understood to involve the granting of a special gift of grace (1 Tim. 4:14, 2 Tim. 1:6; see Rom. 12:5-8). These gifts are given by the risen Christ through the Holy Spirit (1 Cor. 12:4-11, 27-31, Eph. 4:8-12). According to the tradition this special gift of grace was given in no other way and conferred the power to perform validly and efficaciously the sacraments appropriate to the order.[2]

This special gift of grace was also understood in the tradition to confer a special character and a unique ontological status. Augustine spoke of the mark or character of the redeemer which is given to those who are ordained.[3] Thomas Aquinas' editor argued that a special character is imprinted on the soul in each order of ministry.[4] The fifteenth century Council of Florence held that this character was an indelible sign on the soul. Late in the sixteenth century the Anglican theologian Richard Hooker asserted, "Ministerial power is a mark of separation, because it severeth them that have it from other men, and maketh them a special *order* consecrated unto the service of the Most High in things wherewith others may not meddle."[5]

All of these factors, a special inner call from God, a special gift of grace, and the gift of a special character and status constitute a difference between lay and ordained persons in relation to God and thus a theological difference.

No. There is no theological difference between a lay person and an ordained person in the sense of different relation to God. None of the above grounds for such a difference can be sustained.

First, the idea of being called by God to ordination finds no place in the Bible and little in the tradition. In the New Testament being called by God means being called to faith and repentance, to follow Christ, and to membership in the church. "The Bible knows no instance of a man's being called to an earthly profession or trade by God."[6] The interpretation of 1 Corinthians 7:17-24 as an exception to this is a misunderstanding fostered by modern usage.[7] The only clear exception to this is the calling of the apostles including Paul. The apostles were the highest order of ministry in the primitive church, but their title and office ceased with them.

> The title and office of apostle were not transferable and died out with the passing of the original bearers of the name. Whenever it is applied to individuals in later Christian literature, the use of the term is metaphorical. The church has never had apostles in the New Testament sense since the first century.[8]

In later centuries the term "vocation" was applied only to the calling of monks to the religious or monastic life which did not necessarily involve ordination. With very few exceptions in the later middle ages it was not until the Reformation that the idea of vocation of persons to ordination emerged. However, then it was applied to all other "vocations" as well.[9] Therefore, unless it can be argued that the vocation to ordination is essentially different from the vocation of a Christian, say, to the practice of medicine, then it is difficult to see how divine vocation to ordination can be the basis of a theological difference.

In regard to the special gift of grace conferred in ordination, it has to be noted that the clear implication of the relevant New Testament passages is that every Christian is given one or more gifts.[10] So we are not considering a theological difference between those who possess a gift and those who possess no gift, but rather between those who possess one or more gifts and those who possess other gifts. In view of this it would be difficult to argue that the possession of the gift of grace conferred in ordination results in a relation to God different from that of those persons who possess some gifts but not this one.

In regard to the idea that ordination bestows a unique character, the same point needs to be made. The tradition from Augustine on also taught that a special and permanent character was conferred by baptism and confirmation as well as ordination. So we are not dealing with a situation in which some possess a character conferred by grace and others do not, but a situation in which different grace-conferred characters are possessed. It would be difficult to argue that the possession of different grace-conferred characters constitute different relations to God. Furthermore, the idea of a unique character bestowed in ordination has no basis in the Bible. The only unique character referred to in the New Testament is that gained by initiation into the church, the body of Christ. Since Christ is the last Adam, the second man, and the beginning of a new humanity (1 Cor. 15:22, 45, 47), to be incorporated into him is to be a new creation (2 Cor. 5:17, Gal. 6:15). Beside this any other alleged character is insignificant.

The idea that a character bestowed in ordination constitutes a higher order or ontological status was derived from the structure of the Roman civil service class with its *ordines* and was later interpreted by means of the Neo-Platonist scheme of the hierarchy of being involving various levels of power, authority and reality.[11] This idea of ordination is not coherent with the Bible. The general term in the New Testament which was later applied to the ordained ministry is *diakonia* or service. The background of this usage is found in Jesus' teaching about greatness and leadership among his followers. Here he explicitly rejects the model derived from the gentiles in which their rulers "lord it over them and . . . exercise authority over them." In contrast to this the first and the great among his disciples shall be their servant or slave (Mk. 10:42-45 par; see 9:35 par, Jn. 13:14-16). This rules out any concept of ministry or ordination as of a higher order or ontological status.

I conclude from the foregoing analysis that the negative answer is the correct one, that there is no theological difference between a lay person and an ordained person. This of course does not mean that there are not other differences, such as differences in authority and function, and theological differences deriving from sources other than ordination.

Appendix

OUTLINE OF A METHOD FOR THE ANALYSIS AND
RESOLUTION OF THEOLOGICAL QUESTIONS

(Numbers in parentheses refer to the suggestions below.)

1. What is the significance of this question?   (1, 2)
   Is it an important question?
   Why does it interest you?
   What might be the practical results of answering it one way or
   another?
2. How do you interpret the question?   (4, 5, 7)
   What are other possible interpretations of the question?
   What are the key words in the question and what are their possible
   meanings?
   Does the question need rephrasing in the light of your
   interpretation?
3. Is your interpretation of the question a theological question?   (6)
4. What would count as an answer to the question?   (8)
   What are the possible answers to the question?
5. What is your theological norm, criterion or authority?   (12)
6. What is to be your procedure for answering the question?
   (A, B, or C below)
7. Your answer
   A. What is your answer and what are the grounds for it according
      to your norm?   (9)
   B. What is your assessment of each of the possible answers in the
      light of your norm, and which one is the most satisfactory?
      (10)
   C. What are the results of your investigation of your norm on the
      question?
      Which answer do these results support most strongly?   (11)

For further details on such a method of analysis and argument I recom-
mend John Wilson, *Thinking With Concepts,* Stephen E. Toulmin, *The Uses
of Argument,* and John Hospers, *An Introduction to Philosophical Analysis*

(Englewood Cliffs, NJ: Prentice-Hall, 1969). In the course mentioned in the preface I give students quite specific suggestions about how to analyze, clarify, and resolve specific theological questions and about how to write seminar papers summarizing the results of their work. Since they may be helpful for fleshing out the above outline, they are given below.

SUGGESTIONS FOR WRITING SEMINAR PAPERS

1. In choosing a question I suggest that you select one about which you are really curious and in doubt rather than one about which you have a firm conviction. Of course, work on the latter type of question may lead you to change your mind. But the method outlined here is especially valuable for the former kind of question.

2. It is usually a help in clarifying and interpreting the question to explain at the beginning of your paper why you picked the question, why it interests you, and why you think it is important. In order to test the importance of the question you may want to consider what the practical results might be, if any, of answering it one way or another.

3. When you begin to work on a question, resist the temptation to read a lot first. In my own experience this is usually a way to avoid thinking carefully about the question. Thinking is difficult, and we will usually do anything to avoid it. The easiest way to avoid thinking is to read. Before doing any reading you should first write a brief draft of your paper noting the points below. In this way you will discover what questions you may want to pursue in reading. With these questions in mind you will be able to read to some purpose. If you read without any specific purpose, you will probably not learn anything.

4. Consider what possible interpretations the question may have apart from the one which first occurs to you. In this connection it may help to consider various possible meanings of certain key words in the question. For example, the word "necessary" may be understood logically, morally, practically, legally, psychologically, scientifically, or hypothetically.

5. Select an interpretation of the question which seems most appropriate to you. This may be what you believe the questioner had in mind, or, in the case of your own question, what your interest is. Make clear what this interpretation is, perhaps by rephrasing the question.

6. At this point it is important to be sure that the question, or some aspect of it, is a theological question. That is, be sure that it is a question about God or about the world in relation to God. It is sometimes not easy to distinguish a theological question from a historical, psychological, or scientific question, for example. Sometimes

one interpretation of a question is a theological question whereas another interpretation is not.

7. Do not automatically define all terms. Define only those about which there may be some ambiguity and upon which the questions hang. Usually you will not know what terms need to be defined until you have written a draft of the paper. Often the exploration of the ordinary usage of a key word will help to clarify the question, its interpretation, and the possible answers.

8. Consider what would count as an answer to the question. List all the possible answers which occur to you. Others may occur to you in working on the question.

9. Explain how you are going to proceed in answering the question. If you have an intuition about which is the correct answer, one way to proceed is to adopt this answer and try to argue for it.

10. Another way to proceed is to assess each possible answer in turn to determine the strength of the grounds or reasons which can be given for it and how well it stands up under criticism.

11. A third way to proceed is to investigate your theological norm, criterion, or authority on the question and then to determine which of the possible answers is most coherent with the results of your investigation.

12. In assessing an answer or arguing for it the grounds or reasons for or against it will depend upon the theological norm, criterion or authority you have chosen. If, for example, you have decided on Christian experience as your theological norm, then through introspection, interviews, and the exploration of Christian writings you could investigate whether there is any consensus on the question deriving from these sources. If you have chosen the Magisterium of the Roman Catholic Church as your theological authority, then one way to proceed would be to investigate the ways in which the question is dealt with in Denzinger's *Enchiridion Symbolorum.*

13. If, however, you have adopted as your theological criterion the view outlined in chapter 3 of the text, then your procedure might be as follows:

    a. Using the various biblical dictionaries and theologies, such as those listed in the text, investigate whether the question is addressed directly or indirectly by any biblical authors or consensus of biblical authors.

    b. In order to check the results of your investigation of the Bible, or when the results of this investigation are unclear or nil, you should investigate the theological tradition of the church. Using the theological dictionaries and the histories of theology listed in the text investigate whether the question has been addressed directly or indirectly by any council, formulary, or theologian.

   c.   This use of the Bible and the tradition will require that you "translate" the meaning of the text into the contemporary situation. This is an extraordinarily complex process requiring the greatest creativity. You can get an idea of how it might be done by consulting contemporary theologians on the question you are addressing. For a further exploration of this task see my essay "Where Are We in Theology?" and K. Stendahl, "Biblical Theology, Contemporary," *Interpreter's Dictionary of the Bible,* 1:418-32.

14. Do not include anything in your paper which does not clearly contribute to your analysis, answer, or grounds for your answer. Resist the temptation of the term paper syndrome to include everything which you have found in your reading. See how much you can omit rather than how much you can include. Refrain from flowery and pointless introductions. Begin at the top of page one.

15. Be sure to state your conclusion in the form of a direct answer to the question or to your rephrasing of it. You would be surprised how many papers (and theologians!) never explicitly answer the question.

Notes

1 LOCUS AND METHOD

[1] Much of the first part of this chapter was published in somewhat different form in *New Theology No. 9*. ed. Martin E. Marty and Dean G. Peerman (New York: Macmillan, 1972).

[2] The first volume of essays representing this approach was the well-known *New Essay in Philosophical Theology*, ed. Antony Flew and Alasdair MacIntyre (London: SCM, 1955). A complete bibliography is given in Basil Mitchell, ed., *The Philosophy of Religion* (Oxford: Oxford University, 1971).

[3] Cambridge: Cambridge University, 1963.

[4] *The Logic of Scientific Discovery*, pp. 15-16; quoted in E. R. Emmet, *Learning to Philosophize* (New York: Penguin, 1964), p. 20.

[5] Paul Tillich, *Systematic Theology*, 3 vols. (Chicago: University of Chicago, 1951-63), 1:12.

[6] Cambridge: Cambridge University, 1958. See also Chaim Perelman and Lucie Olbrechts-Tyteca, *The New Rhetoric: A Treatise on Argumentation* (South Bend, Ind: University of Notre Dame, 1969), which makes many of the same points as Toulmin but from the point of view of the rhetorical tradition.

[7] See, for example, James L. Golden, Goddwin F. Berquist, and William E. Coleman, *The Rhetoric of Western Thought* (Dubuque: Kendall/Hunt, 1976); Van Austin Harvey, *The Historian and the Believer* (New York: Macmillan, 1966), ch. 2; and David H. Kelsey, *The Uses of Scripture in Recent Theology* (Philadelphia: Fortress, 1975), ch. 6.

[8] *Op. cit.* pp. 104, 105.

[9] *Op. cit.* p. 141.

[10] *Ibid.*, p. 185.

[11] *Ibid.*, p. 190.

[12] *Ibid.*, p. 194.

[13] James Barr, *The Bible in the Modern World* (New York: Harper & Row, 1973), p. 115

2 REVELATION

[1] *Summa Theologiae*, II-II, q. 6, art. 1.

[2] Justin Martyr, *First Apology*, 46; *Second Apology*, 10.

[3] Clement of Alexandria, *Stromateis*, I, 5.

[4] *Institutes of the Christian Religion*, I, iii, iv.

3 AUTHORITY

[1] See, for example, Langdon Gilkey, *Naming the Whirlwind* (Indianapolis: Bobbs-Merrill, 1969), pp. 296-98, 417-19.

[2] See, for example, Tom F. Driver, *Patterns of Grace: Human Experience as Word of God* (New York: Harper & Row, 1977).

[3] *Systematic Theology*, 1:9.

[4] *Ibid.*, pp. 102-05.

[5] See the summary of the biblical evidence in Karl Barth, *Church Dogmatics,* 13 vols. (Edinburgh: T. & T. Clark, 1936-69), I/2:328-31.

[6] *Institutes,* I, ii, 8.

[7] See *Church Dogmatics,* I/2, sect. 17: "The Revelation of God as the Abolition of Religion"; excerpted in my book *Attitudes Toward Other Religions* (New York: Harper & Row, 1969), ch. 4.

[8] *New Essays in Philosophical Theology,* pp. 98–9.

[9] Robert C. Neville, *God the Creator* (Chicago: University of Chicago, 1968), p. 175; see p. 168. See also Gordon D. Kaufman, *An Essay on Theological Method* (Missoula, Mont.: Scholars Press, 1975), pp. 4–7; and Wayne Proudfoot, "Religious Experience, Emotion, and Belief," *Harvard Theological Review* 70 (1977): 343–67.

[10] "Letter of Anselm to Pope Urban II on the Incarnation of the Word," pt. 1, *Library of Christian Classics,* vol. 10, ed. Eugene R. Fairweather (Philadelphia: Westminster, 1956), p. 98.

[11] *Systematic Theology,* 1:42.

[12] See Calvin, *Institutes,* I, ix.

5 GOD

[1] See Edgar Sheffield Brightman, *A Philosophy of Religion* (New York: Prentice-Hall, 1945), chs. 9, 10.

[2] See *Introduction,* pp. 81 ff., and F. R. Tennant, *Philosophical Theology,* 2 vols. (Cambridge: Cambridge University, 1930), 2:166–67.

[3] See *Introduction,* p. 81.

[4] See Clement C. J. Webb, *God and Personality* (New York: Macmillan, 1918), chs. 2, 3.

[5] See William Temple, *Nature, Man and God* (New York: Macmillan, 1951), pp. 202–08.

[6] *Systematic Theology,* 3: 231–37.

[7] "Objectivity in Religion," in *Adventure: The Faith of Science and the Science of Faith* by Burton H. Streeter, et al. (New York: Macmillan, 1928), p. 193. See also W. H. Moberly in *Foundations* by B. H. Streeter et al. (Macmillan, 1920), pp. 501–4.

[8] *The Divine Relativity: A Social Conception of God* (New Haven, CT: Yale University, 1948), pp. 143–44.

[9] *Systematic Theology,* 1:17. See Jn. 1:1–18, Col. 1:15–20.

[10] *Systematic Theology,* 1:174–78, 243–45. For an interpretation in terms of process philosophy, see John B. Cobb, Jr., *A Christian Natural Theology* (Philadelphia: Westminster, 1965), ch. 5.

6 CREATION

[1] See, for example, Morris R. Cohen and Ernest Nagel, *An Introduction to Logic and Scientific Method* (New York: Harcourt, Brace, 1934), ch. 3.

[2] See Augustine's struggle with this issue, *On the Soul and Its Origin,* 1:16–34.

[3] "Does the 'God Who Acts' Really Act?" *Anglican Theological Review* 47 (1965): 79.

[4] "Relativism, Divine Causation, and Biblical Theology," *Encounter* 36 (1975): 347. Both of these essays are reprinted in my book *God's Activity in the World* (Chico, CA: Scholars, 1983).

[5] *Summa Theologiae,* Ia, q. 19, art. 8; *Institutes,* I, xvii, 9.

[6] *Summa Theologiae,* Ia, q. 105, art. 5; see *Summa Contra Gentiles,* III, 70.

[7] *Institutes,* II, iv, 2.

[8] See Gen. 45:5, 8, 50:20, Job 38–41, Ps. 127:1, Prov. 16:1, 9, Isa. 26:12, Mt. 10:29, Acts 2:23, 4:27–28, 1 Cor. 12:6 ("There are varieties of working, but it is the same God who works rather than 'inspires' [RSV] them all in every one."), Phil. 2:13.

[9] See *Introduction,* pp. 113–15; *God's Activity in the World,* passim.; and Ian G. Barbour, *Issues in Science and Religion* (Englewood Cliffs, N.J.: Prentice-Hall, 1966), ch. 13.

[10] Among the many interpretations of process philosophy see, for example, John B. Cobb, Jr., *A Christian Natural Theology* (Philadelphia: Westminster, 1965), chs. 1, 4, 5.

[11] See J. F. Bethune-Baker, *An Introduction to the Early History of Christian Doctrine* (London: Methuen, 1903), pp. 304–5n.

7 PROVIDENCE

[1] For an illuminating discussion of the aspects or dimensions of human life and their relations, see Tillich, *Systematic Theology,* 3:17–28.

[2] *Confessions,* V, 7; *On the Trinity,* III, vi, viii, *City of God,* V, 8.

[3] *Summa Theologiae,* Ia, q. 103–105.

[4] *Institutes,* I, xvi, 3–5; xvii, 6; xviii, 1–3. See also the Heidelberg Catechism, 26–28.

[5] *God Was in Christ* (New York: Scribner, 1948), pp. 111–12.

[6] *Thinking With Concepts,* pp. 96–111.

8 HUMANITY

[1] See Calvin, *Institutes*, I, xv, 1-4.

[2] Ch. 7. Many of the historical references in this chapter are derived from Margaret R. Miles, *Fullness of Life: Historical Foundations for a New Asceticism* (Philadelphia: Westminster, 1981).

[3] *Stromateis*, IV, 3.

[4] *On First Principles*, I, 8.

[5] *On the Resurrection of the Flesh*, 7, 8.

[6] *The City of God*, XV, 7.

[7] *Summa Theologiae*, Ia, q. 75, 76.

[8] See, for example, Charles Davis, *Body as Spirit: The Nature of Religious Feeling* (New York: Seabury, 1976).

[9] See Miles, *Fullness of Life*, pp. 123-24.

[10] *On the Freedom of the Will*, II, xvi, 41.

[11] *Summa Theologiae*, Ia, q. 75, a. 1.

[12] *Institutes*, I, xv, 2-4.

[13] *Systematic Theology*, XXX, 3:11-28. See also Karl Barth, *Church Dogmatics*, III/2, sect. 46; and John B. Cobb, Jr., *A Christian Natural Theology*, ch. 2.

9 SIN

[1] The concept of complementarity is rather complex. For a brief discussion and references, see Ian G. Barbour, *Myths, Models and Paradigms* (London: SCM, 1977), ch. 5.

[2] *Psychotherapy and a Christian View of Man* (New York: Scribner, 1950), p. 104.

[3] See *Introduction*, p. 135.

[4] *On Marriage and Concupiscence*, I, 7 (vi).

[5] *The Denial of Death* (New York: Free Press, 1973), p. 196.

[6] *Beyond Psychology* (New York: Dover, 1958), p. 193; quoted in Becker, op. cit., p. 197.

[7] See *Introduction*, p. 130.

[8] *Ibid.*, p. 137.

[9] See Erik Erikson's concept of basic trust in *Childhood and Society* (New York: W. W. Norton, 1964), pp. 239-43.

10 CHRIST

[1] See *Introduction*, ch. 4.

[2] See *ibid.*, pp. 67-71.

[3] See Jaroslav Pelikan, *The Christian Tradition*, 5 vols. (Chicago: University of Chicago, 1971-), 1:184-86; Tillich, *Systematic Theology*, 3:144-49.

[4] See D. M. Baillie, *God Was in Christ*, pp. 114-32.

11 SALVATION

[1] For a good brief guide to responsible definition see Frederick Ferré, *Basic Modern Philosophy of Religion* (New York: Scribner, 1967), pp. 30-41.

[2] See above pp. 63f.

[3] See, for example, Gustavo Gutierrez, *A Theology of Liberation* (Maryknoll, N.Y.: Orbis, 1973), pp. 165-68.

12 JUSTIFICATION

[1] Session 6, ch. 6.

[2] See *Introduction*, p. 184.

13 ELECTION AND PREDESTINATION

[1] On this issue see Schubert M. Ogden, *Christ Without Myth* (New York: Harper & Row, 1961), pp. 117-25.

[2] See Justin Martyr, *First Apology*, 46; *Second Apology*, 10.

[3] *Summa Contra Gentiles*, I, chs. 2, 3.

[4] *Theological Investigations*, Vol. 5 (New York: Seabury, 1966), p. 127.

[5] See John V. Taylor, "The Theological Basis of Interfaith Dialogue," *Christianity and Other*

Religions: Selected Readings, ed. John Hick and Brian Hebblethwaite (Philadelphia: Fortress, 1980), p. 232.

14 SANCTIFICATION
[1] *Toward a Psychology of Being,* 2d ed. (New York: Van Nostrand Reinhold, 1968), p. 25.
[2] *Ibid.,* p. 26.
[3] *Motivation and Personality,* 2d ed. (New York: Harper & Row, 1970), pp. 268–70.
[4] See above pp. 63f.
[5] See above p. 46.
[6] See above p. 46.
[7] See *God Was in Christ,* pp. 114–18.
[8] See *Motivation and Personality,* p. 168.
[9] See Karl Rahner, "Self-Realization and Taking Up One's Cross," *Theological Investigations,* vol. 9 (London: Darton, Longman, and Todd, 1972), ch. 15.
[10] See the Vatican II Dogmatic Constitution on the Church, II, 16).
[11] See *Introduction,* p. 167.
[12] *Systematic Theology,* 3:241.

15 HISTORY
[1] See *Introduction,* pp. 213f.
[2] See Irenaeus, *Against the Heresies,* IV; Augustine, *City of God,* X, 14.
[3] A clear statement of this answer can be found in Gordon D. Kaufman, *Systematic Theology: A Historicist Perspective* (New York: Scribner, 1968), chs. 19, 22. A quite different version can be found in Pierre Teilhard de Chardin, *The Future of Man* (New York: Harper & Row, 1964), ch. 4.
[4] See, for example, Karl Löwith, *Meaning in History* (Chicago: University of Chicago, 1949), concl.; and Nicholas Berdyaev, *The Meaning of History* (Cleveland: World, 1936), epilogue.
[5] See, for example, Emil Brunner, *Christianity and Civilization* (New York: Scribner, 1948), 1:2–4; and Paul Tillich, *The Protestant Era* (Chicago: University of Chicago, 1948), pp. 262–66.
[6] See Arnold Toynbee, *A Study of History,* Abridgement by D. C. Somervell (New York: Oxford, 1947), pp. 40–41.
[7] For an analysis of the areas in which progress is and is not possible, see Tillich, *Systematic Theology,* 3:333–39.
[8] See Emil Brunner, *Eternal Hope,* (Philadelphia: Westminster, 1954), p. 21; *Revelation and Reason* (Philadelphia: Westminster, 1946), pp. 383–87.

16 ESCHATOLOGY
[1] See *Introduction,* pp. 220f.
[2] See C. F. von Weizsäcker, *The History of Nature* (Chicago: University of Chicago, 1949).
[3] See above, pp. 63f.
[4] *Systematic Theology,* 3:394, 399–401.
[5] *Reaping the Whirlwind* (New York: Seabury, 1976), pp. 297–98.
[6] See, for example, Irenaeus, *Against the Heresies,* V, 36; Augustine, *City of God,* XX, 16, 24; Aquinas, *Summa Theologiae,* suppl., q. 91.
[7] See, for example, Emil Brunner, *Eternal Hope,* ch. 18; Jürgen Moltmann, *Theology of Hope* (New York: Harper & Row, 1967), pp. 136f, 214f; Kaufman, *Systematic Theology,* pp. 320–23. The clearest statement of the contradictory character of the relation of theology and science on this issue is found in Karl Heim, *The World: Its Creation and Consummation* (Edinburgh: Oliver and Boyd, 1962).
[8] See *The Phenomenon of Man* (New York: Harper & Row, 1959), pp. 271f.
[9] See *The Future of Man,* pp. 122f.
[10] See *Introduction,* pp. 101f.

17 CHURCH
[1] See, for example, Robert A. Evans and Thomas D. Parker, eds. *Christian Theology: A Case Method Approach* (New York: Harper & Row, 1976), sect. 7.
[2] *The Church for Others* (Geneva: World Council of Churches, 1967), p. 18.

18 SACRAMENTS
¹ See *Book of Common Prayer,* p. 298.
² Session 6, ch. 6.
³ *Against Marcion,* I, 28.

19 WORSHIP
¹ See *Introduction,* pp. 261–64.
² See Didache, XIV, 1; Ignatius, *Philad.*, 4; Justin, *Dialogue,* CXVII, 1; Irenaeus, *Against the Heresies,* IV, xvii, 5.
³ See, for example, the *Acta SS. Saturnini,* excerpted by B. J. Kidd, ed., *Documents Illustrative of the History of the Church,* vol. 1 (London: SPCK, 1920), no. 172.

20 MINISTRY
¹ In this chapter I am following more closely the procedures suggested by John Wilson in his book *Thinking With Concepts.*
² See, for example, Thomas Aquinas, *Summa Theologiae,* Suppl., q. 35, a. 1.
³ *Epistle* 185, 23.
⁴ *Summa Theologiae,* Suppl., q. 35, a. 2.
⁵ *Laws of Ecclesiastical Polity,* V, 77, 2.
⁶ Alan Richardson, *The Biblical Doctrine of Work* (London: SCM, 1952), p. 33.
⁷ See K. L. Schmidt, *"klesis,"* *Theological Dictionary of the New Testament,* ed. G. Kittel, 9 vols. (Grand Rapids: Eerdmans, 1964–74), 3:491n.
⁸ M. H. Shepherd, Jr., "Apostle," *The Interpreter's Dictionary of the Bible,* 4 vols. (New York: Abington, 1962), 1:172a.
⁹ See the definitive study by Karl Holl, "Die Geschichte des Worts Beruf," *Gesammelte Aufsätze zur Kirchengeschichte,* 3 vols. (Tübingen: Mohr, 1928), 3:189–219.
¹⁰ See E. Andrews, *Interpreter's Dictionary of the Bible,* 4:435a.
¹¹ See Thomas Aquinas, *Summa Theologiae,* Suppl., q. 34, a. 1, and the reference there to Dionysius the Areopagite.